Collins

need to know?

Islam

Ruqaiyyah Waris Maqsood

Collins

First published in 2008 by Collins
an imprint of
HarperCollins Publishers
77–85 Fulham Palace Road
London W6 8JB

www.collins.co.uk

A catalogue record for this book is available from
the British Library

Editor: Grapevine Publishing Services Ltd
Design: Delineate Ltd
Series design: Mark Thomson
Front cover photograph: Getty Images
Back cover photograph: iStockPhoto

All photographs inside the book are by Peter Sanders
(www.petersanders.co.uk) except for pages 68, 147
and 165 which are by Ruqaiyyah Waris Maqsood and
page 156 which is by Chris Bradley.

ISBN 978-0-00-727877-0

Printed and bound by Printing Express Ltd,
Hong Kong

Contents

Introduction 6

1 **The Prophet Muhammad** 8

2 **The Qur'an** 30

3 **What Muslims believe** 46

4 **What Muslims do** 62

5 **Where Muslims worship** 90

6 **Islamic law** 100

7 **The Islamic world view** 112

8 **The history of Islam** 132

9 **Islamic heritage** 152

10 **Issues for today** 176

Glossary 189

Index 191

Introduction

Islam is the faith or belief that there *is* a God, and that He chose the Arab merchant Muhammad b. Abdullah of the Banu Quraysh (570–632 CE) to be His Messenger.

The word Muslims use for God is Allah – which is not so much a name as a description of a quality of Being; it means the Absolute, the Almighty, the Supreme.

When Muhammad was 40 years old, a visionary experience of the angel Jibril (Gabriel) called him to be God's messenger. From that moment on his life was not his own, his privacy sacrificed so that everything he said and did could set the pattern for others and show them how they should live.

For the next 23 years his family and companions bore witness to the constant stream of communications brought to him from the Unseen, messages dealing with every aspect of life from important matters to intimate and seemingly trivial details. He memorized each revelation, sometimes lengthy passages, sometimes just a few words, and dictated everything to others once the visitation had ceased.

From rejection, ridicule and persecution in his own town, he became the King of Madinah, and by the end of his life had unified the whole of Arabia under one rule. He was one of the most famous people on earth, receiving visitors and tributes from all over the known world. He was probably the most loved and meticulously observed ruler and religious guide of history.

The way of life he followed is indicated by the word 'islam' which means 'to submit'. Those who practise Islam are known as Muslims – people who have made the commitment to hand over their lives to the disciplined way based on love and obedience to the will of God as revealed in the revelations Muhammad received, the collection known as the Qur'an. Over the last 14 centuries Islam has fashioned the faith, morality and culture of Muslims all over the world, and it is at present the world's fastest-growing faith.

The aim of this book is to explain the principles of Islam and to show how Muslims strive to bring God-consciousness (*taqwa*) into every area of their daily lives, from the important and profound to the mundane and simple tasks; and in this devotion and urge to serve, striving for the greater pleasure of their Lord, they find their own fulfillment and happiness.

Each chapter in this book is underpinned by the words of the Qur'an and the teachings of Muhammad himself, for they are the basis of Islam.

Note

Some names have variant spellings. The following forms are used in this book: Muhammad (= Mohammed), Makkah (= Mecca), Madinah (= Medina), Qur'an (= Koran).

1 The Prophet Muhammad

The Prophet Muhammad was a man specially
selected by God to communicate His messages
to humanity. For the 23 years of his mission he
lived in almost continuous prayer, guided day
by day by the presence of the angel Jibril
(Gabriel). He was to show God's will through
the way he lived his life, with nobility, honesty,
generosity, compassion, justice, humility,
tenderness, courage and determination. He
lived, loved, fought, suffered, knew joy, sorrow
and frustration – but after his calling he was
forever conscious of divine guidance and the
responsibility laid upon him.

The Prophet Muhammad

This chapter tells the remarkable story of the Prophet, from penniless orphan to ruler of Madinah and all Arabia.

did you know?

Muslims often prefer to use the neutral dating abbreviation CE (Christian Era) rather than AD (Anno Domini, 'In the year of Our Lord').

The years of preparation

Arabia in the 7th century CE had a mixed population of Jews, Christians and pagans. Many were expecting the imminent arrival of another messenger from God like Abraham or Moses, the prophets of old, to ratify the previous revelations, set the standard that would determine what was true or false in their beliefs and documents, and declare God's teaching without ambiguity, so that all people could make an informed choice as to whether to accept and live by God's will. Arabic sources suggested this messenger would have the name of Ahmad. Muslims believe that this prophet was Muhammad.

For the most part, Arabia consisted of scorched, barren deserts, with regions of fertile oases. The centres of population were on the main trade routes that crossed the territory, linking the great cities and permitting the transportation of goods from China and India to Egypt, Africa and across the Mediterranean Sea.

The 'fertile crescent' to the north of Arabia followed the courses of the great rivers Tigris, Euphrates and Jordan. The western coast of the Mediterranean was the region where Abraham, the patriarch of both Arabs and Jews, had led his people from Ur (near Basra in Iraq) via Haran, where biblical history had been played out, and where Jesus had lived and preached.

Page 8: Courtyard of the Great Mosque, Damascus, Syria.

Christianity in various forms had spread throughout what had been the Roman Empire, which was ruled from Byzantium (Constantinople, now Istanbul) by the Christian emperor Heraclius. Missionary monks had introduced Christianity all over Arabia, and many tribes had accepted either Christianity or Judaism.

There was no central government in Arabia, but some regions had kings; elsewhere, independent tribal chieftains gained power through wealth, prestige or exploits in battle, and ruled their own peoples. Many led nomadic lives, seeking out vegetation for their livestock, and settlements were defended zealously. Passage through Arabia was dangerous and required covenants, deals and payment of protection money. Without this, travellers were considered fair game, and many ended up in the slave market. Life was precarious, and it was normal for men to have as many wives and children as they could afford. Some women also practised polygamy, and maintained a settled household that entertained a selection of nomadic husbands.

Makkah and the Ka'bah

The city of Makkah was in barren, waterless territory, but its population had burgeoned because for over 2000 years a very special shrine had been venerated there – the Ka'bah, originally dedicated to the One True God. Abraham had found it in a damaged state and rebuilt it, at God's command, on the same foundations. However, most Arabians worshipped idols, and over the centuries monotheism at the Ka'bah had been compromised by a huge collection

must know

All the quotations from the Prophet given in this book are taken from the *hadith* collections, the memorized records of things he said and did (see box on p. 102). Quotations in italics are from the Qur'an itself (the revealed words of God).

of cultic objects placed there. Three months of the year were regarded as 'sacred truce' months devoted to the gods, and in the month dedicated to a pilgrimage known as a Hajj, devout pagans came hundreds of miles to visit the Ka'bah, encircle it and perform sacrifices.

Arabs who clung to the belief in One God were known as *hanifs*, and longed for the day the Ka'bah could be restored to its original purity. One of these *hanifs* was Abdu'l Muttalib, chief of the Quraysh and Guardian of the Ka'bah. The Prophet Muhammad, born in *c.* 570, was his grandson.

Muhammad's early years

Muhammad's father, Abdullah, died before he was born, and his mother, Aminah, when he was only six years old. His grandfather took custody of him but died two years later, and it was his uncle Abu Talib, a trader, who raised him to manhood.

From the age of 12 Muhammad, along with his best friend, Abu Bakr, accompanied Abu Talib on his journeys from Makkah to Damascus. The boy's honesty and reliability earned him the nickname 'al-Amin', or 'Trustworthy One'. He was observed with some excitement by more than one Christian monk on these travels, who prophesied his future great significance.

He gained his first experience of tribal warfare by the age of 14, and at 16 was a young knight in an order of chivalry founded by another of his uncles – a group dedicated to defending the weak and downtrodden wherever they came across corruption, bullying and oppression of those who could not defend themselves against the arrogant and powerful. Muhammad was famed for his decency, his bashfulness and chastity (not common virtues in those days), his open-heartedness and chivalry, and as he reached adulthood, his keen, practical wisdom.

Marriage to Khadijah

Muhammad had hoped to marry his cousin, but permission was refused. Instead, he became caravan-leader for a wealthy trader, Khadijah bint Khuwaylid, famed as one of the most beautiful women of Makkah. Khadijah had already been married (and widowed) twice, and had at least four children when, in 595, at the age of 40, she proposed to Muhammad, who was still single at 25 years old, and much too shy to ask her.

Theirs was a famous love-match, and it took Muhammad from modest circumstances to wealth. He became a respected tribal elder, noted for his kindness and piety. Khadijah was his only life-partner until her death 25 years later, and they produced a family of at least six children, two boys (Qasim and Abdullah) who died in infancy, and four girls (Zaynab, Ruqaiyyah, Umm Kulthum and Fatimah). They also fostered two boys – the teenage Zayd ibn Harithah (a slave who had been captured in a raid and given to Khadijah), and Abu Talib's youngest son, Ali, who came to live with them from the age of four.

His call to prophethood

In 610, when Muhammad was 40, something happened that changed his life forever. He had taken up his grandfather's custom of spending one month of the year in solitary contemplation in a cave at the top of the nearby Mount Hira, with provisions sent daily from his household. One night, towards the end of the month, he experienced a presence with him in the cave, which identified itself as the angel Jibril, the angel God used to communicate revelations to humanity.

He was shown a scroll upon which were written words that he could not read, his body felt gripped and crushed until he feared he would die, and twice he heard a voice command him, 'Recite!' He protested that he could not do so. The third

Information about the
Prophet comes from the
thousands of *hadiths*,
which give insight into his
life and character, and
several early biographies
and lists of military
expeditions and martyrs.
The earliest biography
was by Ibn Ishaq, some
120 years after the
Prophet's death.

time, he was given knowledge of the first words of
the message he had been ordered to go and repeat
to others. Then he found himself once more alone in
the cave, in a state of shock.

The night on which the first revelation was given
is known as 'Laylat ul-Qadr', or 'Night of Power'. Its
date is not known for certain, but was on one of the
'odd' dates towards the end of the Arab lunar month
of Ramadan.

Back home, Muhammad saw the angel again. At
first terrified that he had been deceived and
possessed by some evil supernatural entity, he was
reassured by Khadijah and her Christian cousin
Waraqah (famed for translating a Gospel into Arabic)
that a man of his character could not be susceptible
to such things. He must have been called by God to
be His messenger, a prophet.

Having accepted the possibility of his calling,
Muhammad experienced nothing further for about
two years. Perplexed and full of anxiety, he returned
to the mountain once more. At last, the angel came
again, with these famous words of comfort: '*By the
glorious light of morning, and by the stillness of night
– your Lord has never forsaken you, and He is not
angry with you. Be certain – your future will be better
for you than your past, and in the end God will be
kind to you and you will be satisfied. Did He not find
you an orphan, and gave you a home? Did He not
find you lost and wandering, and showed you the
way? Did He not find you in great need, and took care
of you? As for you, therefore, never wrong the
orphans, nor turn away those that ask your help;
spread and increase your Lord's blessings.*' (Surah
93.1-11)

From that moment on, Muhammad received visitations for the rest of his life. The angel might come at any moment, day or night, and in order that everything he said and did could become the pattern for others, he no longer enjoyed any privacy.

Accepting this role never once affected Muhammad's humility. He knew he was vitally important as the means of making the Divine Words known to humanity – but he also knew he was entirely dependent upon God's will. If God chose to be silent, there was nothing he could do.

Muhammad's mission in Makkah

At first Muhammad only spoke about his experiences to his immediate family and close friends. However, the visitations did not necessarily take place privately. Before long, many had witnessed the trance-like state that came over him: he would be stopped abruptly from doing whatever he was doing, his breathing would change, and he would be incapable of anything else until the revelation ceased.

Sometimes Muhammad saw the angel, which could take any form and sometimes came as a handsome man; other times he heard a voice, either speaking to him or in his mind. Sometimes, if he felt warning signs, he had time to lie down wrapped in his cloak. Sometimes it happened without any warning. It could be a specific reply to a question that had been troubling him, perhaps for some time. Sometimes others present observed him looking fixedly at something they could not see, or speaking to an invisible visitor. Occasionally he seemed to lose consciousness. Frequently he became soaked in a profuse sweat. He said, 'Not once did I receive a

Raising outstretched open palms is the traditional position for private prayers.

revelation without thinking that my soul had been torn away.'

When the contact ceased, he would carefully repeat the words he had been given, making sure they were accurately recorded as promptly as possible on whatever writing materials were to hand. It soon became usual practice to have such things ready at all times, along with someone who could act as scribe for him. There was an atmosphere of urgency and excitement as section by section God gave him direct guidance for every aspect of life.

The messages were intended to confirm previously revealed scriptures and be a guidance and blessing to all those who chose to accept them, but Muhammad did not have the right to try to coerce people to believe. '*This is the Truth from your Lord,*' the angel told him. '*Whoever will believe, let them believe, and whoever will, let them disbelieve.*' (Surah 18-29)

The dramatic nature of the Prophet's divine seizures naturally led sceptics to suppose he might have suffered from epilepsy, or was being possessed by some evil spirit, or had become a *kahin* (spiritual poet). Others suggested he had gone mad, or had decided to perpetrate this peculiar fraud on the gullible for purposes of his own. To reassure him that he was not mad or possessed, Muhammad received several revelations that were directed to him personally.

The private stage of his mission came to an abrupt end when he was ordered to make his teaching public. He summoned the Quraysh chiefs to a feast, and asked if they would believe him if he told them there was an enemy army on the far side of the hill. They all agreed that as he never lied, they would do so. He launched into his first public sermon, which summed up his message: 'I am asking you to worship the One Almighty God!' he cried. 'Give up your worship of idols, and your evil and corrupt practices. If you do this, you will find success; but if you refuse, you will suffer badly for it, and on the Day of Judgement it will be too late for you to save yourselves! O Quraysh, rescue yourselves from the Fire!'

The chiefs laughed at him and left. Undaunted, he invited them again the next day and urged them to believe, but they remained embarrassed and hostile. No one responded. As the awkward silence lengthened it was too much for Ali. He stood up and marched over defiantly to stand alongside Muhammad. 'O Prophet of Allah,' he said boldly, glaring at his uncles, '*I* will be your helper.' Needless to say, they laughed at him, too.

Reaction to his message

Reaction was predictable. People were either entirely convinced of the truth of his calling, or horrified by the implications of his claims, which challenged their pagan ancestral religion and customs. They did their best to silence him. The appeal of his message to fervent youngsters, and to many womenfolk and slaves (now to be treated as individuals whose morality and piety might even make them superior to their menfolk) alarmed their families and households. He was accused of disrupting families, corrupting the minds of the youth and making women and slaves rebellious. His own family was split down the middle. Two of his daughters were married to the sons of another uncle, Abu Lahab. They were divorced and sent back to him.

must know

The very first converts were Khadijah and the 10-year-old Ali. The first adult male converts were Muhammad's best friend, the merchant Abu Bakr, and his fostered son Zayd, followed within days by many others who knew him best. Their excited reports of what had happened to Muhammad spread like wildfire.

must know

The word 'Muslim' means 'those who accept and submit to the will of God', and therefore enter the state of *tasleem*, or 'being in Islam'.

Muhammad was asking a lot of them, without proof. Why didn't he perform a miracle, as Jesus had done? Muhammad insisted that receiving the words of God *was* his miracle. When it became obvious that he was not going to give up, some outraged Makkans turned from ridicule to hostility, although they did not dare kill him because he was still under the protection of his highly respected uncle, Abu Talib.

Many of his followers did not enjoy the same level of protection, however. Muslims were chained, tied up and beaten (often by their own relatives), and kept without food, drink or sleep. They were stoned, pelted with filth and offal, shunned and ignored, or bullied and threatened. Unable to defend them-selves, slaves suffered terribly. Some, like the Abyssinian slave Bilal, were staked out in the blazing sun and left to die.

Many Muslims were extremely fervent in defence of their new cause. The Prophet urged them not to harbour bitter, hateful or vengeful thoughts, but to accept with courage, patience, dignity and restraint all the persecution flung at them for God's sake. He assured them that God would grant them the strength to cope. He told them he had been commanded to deal gently with disbelievers, and give them time to change their minds.

Some converts were influential people, however, such as the wealthy merchants Uthman ibn Affan, who married the Prophet's divorced daughter Ruqaiyyah (and later the other daughter too), Umar ibn Khattab, and Abu Bakr, who bought and freed Bilal as well as many other slaves. A rich landowner, Arqam, donated his house for use as the Muslim headquarters.

Muhammad leaves Makkah

Muhammad's enemies organized a boycott of his entire clan, forced them out of Makkah and blockaded them in a barren valley for three years. There, they struggled to stave off starvation – helped by a few brave souls who provisioned them in secret. Abu Bakr, for example, devoted his entire fortune to keeping them alive and was himself reduced to poverty. Some went as refugees to Abyssinia, where they were helped by the Negus Abrahah, a Christian king who later converted to Islam.

The boycott ended, but there were more troubles to come. In 619 both Khadijah and Abu Talib died. No longer protected by this highly respected tribal leader, Muhammad was in even more danger. When he tried preaching in the nearby city of Taif he was stoned out of town. Muhammad's sadness at the death of his wife was lifted by the bravery and love of his youngest daughter Fatimah (who became known as 'Umm Abiha', or 'Mother of her father'), and Ali. After two years he was persuaded to remarry, and took two wives – the widow Sawdah (one of the earliest converts to Islam) and Abu Bakr's little daughter Aishah, who had been engaged almost since birth to a non-Muslim who now repudiated her. She was as yet too young for physical marriage.

Muhammad's ascension

One night the Prophet was given another life-changing experience. The angel Jibril roused him from sleep and transported him (whether by vision or miracle) to Jerusalem on a winged creature known as a *buraq*. From there, he was allowed a glimpse of Hell before ascending through the seven heavens, during

must know

The first martyr of Islam, who was staked out and then speared, was an elderly slave-woman called Sumayyah.

must know

Great love developed
between the Prophet
and his young wife
Aishah. She is venerated
as one of the most
authoritative witnesses
of Muhammad's life, and
was consulted as a
leading scholar of Islam

which experience he met and spoke to several of the
prophets of old, including Abraham and Moses, and
to Jesus. Muhammad discussed with Moses how
many times a day a Muslim should pray. The
number was fixed at five, and this has remained
Muslim practice ever since.

He approached the Throne of God, the highest
spiritual state attainable, but neither he nor the
angel was able to see God since He was surrounded
by incandescent light. On returning to his normal
state, Muhammad had renewed strength and hope.

Muhammad, ruler of Madinah

In those same years that the growing Muslim
community was being persecuted in Makkah, Islam
was spreading amongst the people of the wealthy
oasis-town of Yathrib, some 338 km to the north,
with its mixed population of Arabs and Jews. There
had been years of rivalry and warfare between these
tribes, and a group of leaders hoped to bring peace
by inviting Muhammad to become their ruler. While
on pilgrimage to the Ka'bah, many of them swore a
secret pact of allegiance to the Prophet.

The Hijrah: migration to Madinah

Once the pact was agreed, Makkan Muslims began
to leave their homes and migrate to Yathrib.
Muhammad left in 622, one of the last to go.
Knowing his enemies would try to hunt him down
the moment he entered the desert, he slipped away,
accompanied by Abu Bakr, leaving Ali to bring his
family to Madinah unendangered by his presence.

Muhammad arrived to a tumultuous welcome.
Like the other emigrants, he and his family were

did you know?

Muhammad's ascension was not the taking up of his body into Heaven after his death (as happened to Jesus) but occurred during his lifetime. The night is called 'Laylat ul-Miraj', or 'Night of Ascent', and because of Muhammad's experience Muslims regard Jerusalem as their third holiest city. Muhammad's body lies buried in Madinah.

The Dome of the Rock on the site of the Temple of Jerusalem, the first dome built in Islam (see p. 95).

billeted amongst converted Madinan volunteers while he and his companions cleared the ground and built little houses alongside the large enclosed space where his mosque was set up.

The Muslims who emigrated there were known as *Muhajirun* (i.e., those who had made the *hijrah* to Madinah). Having left all behind, most were as destitute as refugees. The Muslims of Yathrib who took them into their homes and provisioned them until they found their feet were called *Ansar* ('Helpers'). The Prophet created a brotherhood union with an *Ansar* for every *Muhajirun*.

must know

A mosque (Ar. *masjid*, from the word *sajada*, 'to bow down') is a Muslim place of prayer. Prayer involves kneeling on the earth and touching the ground with the forehead.

The Muslim state and charter

At this stage, Madinah's population of around 10,000 included only a few hundred Muslims. About half its citizens were Jews, and the rest were pagan idol-worshippers, but they all swore fealty to a charter, the Constitution of Madinah, which committed them to mutual cooperation. This was possibly the world's first written constitution.

This important document did not use the term Islamic or Muslim state, but it did lay down the principles for such a society – including justice, brotherhood and unity of believers, equality for all its members and protection against oppression, freedom of religion for those who were not Muslim, encouragement of high moral conduct, strict adherence to pacts entered into between parties, and consultation as a method of government.

Muhammad hoped the Jews would accept him as a prophet. Some did, but many could not take his teachings as new scripture after their revelation of the Torah (the Jewish Scriptures). The wealthy Rabbi Mukhayriq, however, made him his heir.

Muhammad, ruler of Madinah

Although now respected and honoured as ruler of Madinah, the Prophet never accepted the title of king. He believed that there was no king but God, and refused to adopt any of the trappings of temporal sovereignty. Far from seeking to be raised above his subjects, he built no palaces and had no throne, but was content to sit on the floor in total simplicity. 'I eat as a slave eats,' he said, 'and I sit as a slave sits. I am only a slave.' Even when he became exceedingly wealthy through spoils and tributes, he

continued to live like a poor man and distributed the
wealth to needy subjects. His home, alongside the
mosque, was a row of tiny dwellings so small you
could touch their roofs, occupied by his wives. 'Shall I
tell you about the people of Paradise?' he once said.
'They consist of obscure, unimportant and humble
people who keep their word. And shall I tell you about
the people of the Fire? They consist of cruel, violent,
proud and conceited people.'

The life of prayer

The lives of the Prophet and his Companions were
passed in prayer and study, looking out for opportunities to help each other in times of hardship. He urged
his followers to show practical charity, without
thinking of reward. 'Feed the destitute, the orphan
and the prisoner for the love of Allah, saying – "We
feed you for God's sake alone, and desire no reward
from you, nor thanks."'

   He disliked extremism, and social withdrawal, and
rebuked his followers if he felt they were neglecting
their spouses or families. Extremism encouraged
people to turn their backs on their social responsibili-
ties and commitments in order to retreat into a world
of excessive devotions and asceticism, the excuse
being that they did what they did purely for love of
Allah. 'Muslims who live in the midst of society and
bear with patience the afflictions that come their way
are better than those who shun society and cannot
bear any wrong done to them,' he said.

Why did Muhammad fight wars?

The Prophet hated war and bloodshed, but his Makkan
enemies had no intention of letting him establish his

kingdom in peace. Furious that so many influential citizens had been 'corrupted' and had deserted Makkah, they promptly confiscated everything the *Muhajirun* had been obliged to leave behind.

In 624 the Prophet's rag-tag army of 400, with few weapons, little armour and a couple of horses between them, found themselves facing 1000 heavily armed Makkans (many of them their own relatives, a matter of great distress) at Badr. To everyone's surprise, the Makkans were defeated in the one-day battle, with 70 Makkans slain but only 14 Muslims. Ali distinguished himself as a great warrior, and not long after this battle he and the Prophet's daughter Fatimah were married.

In the reprisal Battle of Uhud in 625, only 22 Makkans were killed, as opposed to about 70 Muslims. Muslim men were urged to take their widows and children into their own households. The Prophet himself took in three widows and their children – Umar's daughter Hafsah, his cousin Umm Salamah, and a more distant relative, Zaynab bint Khuzaymah.

Trouble flared with some of the influential Jewish citizens, which ended with one tribe abandoning the treaty and leaving Madinah. In 627 the Makkans, led by the famous warrior Khalid ibn Walid, gathered a huge army of 10,000 and marched on Madinah, but were held off by a massive trench hastily excavated around the parts of the city that were susceptible to attack. This time the Muslims were betrayed by the Jewish tribe of Banu Qurayzah, who deliberately left their quarter undefended to allow the enemy to surge into Madinah and overrun it. Many were therefore executed after the Muslim victory, including the Rabbi Kinanah – whose widow

Safiyyah the Prophet married, at her request. The Prophet might have spared them, but judgement was left in the hands of one of their own confederates, who sentenced them according to their own law.

In 628 Muhammad indicated his desire for peace by leading 1400 unarmed Muslim pilgrims to Makkah. They were refused entry to the city, but a truce was negotiated and they made their sacrifices at their camp, Hudaybiyah. The following year an even larger band went to Makkah, and this time the Makkans filed out of the city to avoid confrontation, allowing them access while they watched from the hills. The enemy commander Khalid, impressed by the Muslim honesty and discipline, changed sides and joined Islam.

The Year of the Deputations

The Prophet was by now a famous man. Hundreds of delegations came to visit him, and many declared allegiance. Letters went from Muhammad to surrounding rulers inviting them to accept Islam, and many did (including two Christian archbishops but not, notably, the Emperor of Persia, who responded savagely). Some signed treaties even if they did not accept Islam. Nobody was forced to become Muslim. The system was that if they swore allegiance they would be protected in their own faiths but had to pay a tax, the *jizya* (in place of the *zakah*, which was compulsory for Muslims).

Victory over Makkah

In 629 some Makkans broke their truce and attacked one of the converted Arab tribes. The Prophet promptly marched on Makkah with his now huge

must know

The Prophet's chief scribe was Zayd ibn Thabit, who joined his household from the age of 12, and when only 16 learned enough Hebrew and Syriac to translate documents and draft letters, some of which still exist. Later, he also learned Persian and Coptic.

army – but they had orders not to fight unless they were absolutely forced to. Those who did not oppose them were not to be harmed, and to the amazement of the Makkans there was no slaughter, rape or pillage. The *Muhajirun* were not even permitted to take back the homes they had left.

The Prophet entered the Ka'bah shrine and destroyed all the idols. His Madinah followers were worried that he might now want to leave them and return to his old home, but he assured them that his heart was theirs, and he would stay with them until he passed away.

Gradually all the tribes either accepted Islam, or swore loyalty to the Prophet's State and agreed to abide by his law.

The death of the Prophet

In March 632 the Prophet led some 140,000 pilgrims to Makkah, during which all the Islamic rules for Hajj – followed by Muslims to this day – were revealed to him. Pagans were now forbidden access to the Ka'bah, and Makkah became a city dedicated to God alone. After a very moving sermon of farewell, in which he told them of his premonition that he would never be among them again, the Prophet returned to Madinah, and *en route* was visited by the angel for the last time. The Qur'an was complete.

Shi'ite Muslims strongly maintain that he called a halt for a vast gathering at Ghadir Khumm, where he announced that his successor should be Ali.

Back in Madinah, the Prophet suddenly fell ill, and within days became too weak to lead the prayers. He insisted that his place should be taken by his dear friend, Abu Bakr. To the utter shock of the faithful, he passed away at the age of 63, in the arms of his wife Aishah.

Aishah said of him, 'He never abused or spoke ill of anybody. He forgave faults and refrained from retaliation. He never thought of taking personal revenge, forgave non-believing enemies promptly on their conversion to Islam; never fought on personal grounds; took an interest in his household affairs; condemned vendettas and blood-feuds; and never beat anyone, not even a slave.'

Ali was once asked how great was the love of the Companions for their Prophet. 'By Allah,' he replied, 'to us the Prophet was dearer than our riches, our children and our mothers, more dear than a drink of cold water at the time of severest thirst.'

The Sunnah: Muhammad's example

Devout Muslims do their utmost to follow his way of life and example in their own lives, even in details of how to eat, drink, fulfil nature's functions, dress, behave, and carry out their duties. His example is known as the 'Sunnah'.

• Some Muslims regard everything he did as compulsory for all Muslims.

• Others take the view that it is indeed good to follow his personal practice but it is not compulsory unless specifically stated in the Qur'an.

• Others insist that most important is the *principle* behind the practice. For example, *modesty* was more important than any *imitated style* of clothing.

'His way of life,' said Aishah, '*is* the Qur'an. He is pleased by what it finds pleasing, and angry according to what it finds hateful.'

Muslims do *not* worship the Prophet Muhammad, and regard it as blasphemy to do so. As a messenger of God, his duty was to preach and warn, but no more. He insisted that he should never be regarded as anything other than a human being, albeit a very special one, and thought it improper to try to judge which prophet was the greatest of all. Jesus was considered a prophet by Muslims, renowned as the virgin-born and miracle-worker, and Muhammad was the *last*, often referred to as the 'Seal of the Prophets'.

Some Muslims do maintain that the Prophet was perfect and incapable of human error, but Muhammad actually insisted that

The Prophet's Mosque, Madinah. The green dome is directly over the Prophet's tomb.

must know

The Shi'ites (or Shi'a) are Muslims who separated from the mainstream of Islam following the death of the Prophet. Their correct name is Shi'at Ali, or supporters of Ali in his claim to be the Prophet's successor (rather than Abu Bakr).

when he spoke and made judgements without divine guidance he was subject to the normal limitations of knowledge and skill. 'I am only a human being to whom people come to settle disputes,' he said. 'One might be more eloquent than the other in presenting his case, and I might consider him truthful and pass a judgement in his favour. If ever I do so in favour of someone who is *not* in the right, then what he gains from it will be a piece of the Fire.'

He never claimed any esoteric knowledge except that which Allah chose to reveal to him, pointing out that if he had had access to advantageous information he could have acquired enormous benefits for himself and avoided harmful consequences.

Some have also assumed that the Prophet was without sin, but he said: 'By Allah! I ask for God's forgiveness and turn to Him in repentance more than 70 times a day.' One of his habits when leaving a house was to raise his eyes to the sky and pray: 'O Allah, I seek refuge in You lest I stray or lead others astray, or cause injustice, or suffer injustice, or do wrong, or have wrong done to me.'

Miracles were certainly recorded of him during his lifetime, but he taught that everything was dependent upon the will and power of Allah, and the only miracle of importance was the revelation to him of the Qur'an.

Criticism of the Prophet in some Islamic societies has been (wrongly) equated with blasphemy, and might even bring with it the threat of prison or even the death penalty. This has not deterred non-Muslims from insulting him throughout history. In the Middle Ages Muhammad was thought of as an idol to whom Muslims prayed, or one of the heathen gods or demons. He was referred to as 'Mahound' ('Devil Incarnate'), and it was claimed he died in the year 666 (the number of the Beast). Later attacks focused on presenting him as a cunning, ambitious, voluptuous and self-seeking impostor. Kinder detractors assumed he was absolutely sincere, but deluded.

Some people have supposed the Prophet to have been a severe, austere man, but in fact – as one Companion said of him – 'I have seen no person smiling more than the Messenger of Allah.' One little girl, Rubayyi, described the Prophet as being 'as if the sun came out'.

want to know more?

• A. Guillaume, *The Life of Muhammad*, Oxford University Press, 1955
• K. Armstrong, *Muhammad: A Biography of the Prophet*, HarperOne, 1993
• M. Haykal, *The Life of Muhammad*, New American Trust Publications, 1976

2 The Qur'an

The Qur'an is the Holy Book of Islam. Muslims
treasure the text in its original Arabic as the
literal word of God, the last of God's books
revealed to humanity, transmitted by the
Prophet Muhammad, section by section,
through the angel Jibril (Gabriel) over a period
of almost 23 years (610-32). It lays down the
guidelines within which they may order their
lives in keeping with God's will, should they
choose to do so.

The Qur'an

This chapter explains the origin, format, purpose and presentation of the scriptures of Islam.

The 'Mother of Books' (Umm al-Kitab)

The Qur'an is not a book written *by* Muhammad, a product of his own mind or talents. Not one word was actually written by the Prophet's own hand. It is often claimed that he could not read or write, although this is disputed. In his time, writing was considered something wealthy people paid scribes to do.

It most certainly is not a collection of the sayings of Muhammad – which were also highly revered. These were recorded meticulously, kept quite separate, and are known as the *hadiths*. The Qur'an is about the same length as the Christian New Testament, but the *hadiths* run to many volumes and fill bookshelves.

The Qur'an cannot be broken down into a work compiled from various source-materials. The entire content is prophecy in the true sense of the word: transmitted through a prophet. It is a difficult book for non-Muslims to read and appreciate properly, for several reasons:
• There is no real beginning or end, and it does not flow in a chronological sequence.
• It was revealed in Arabic, and therefore needs translating, but its form of Arabic is so loaded that it is virtually impossible to grasp its full meaning.
• It only makes full sense if one knows the background to the verses, when and why they were revealed, the range of possible meanings, etc.

Page 30: Arches of the Mezquita, Córdoba, Spain.

A reader therefore needs copious footnotes or a commentary.

The fate of the texts of messages sent by God to previous prophets had been precarious, so this time accurate preservation was of paramount importance, and achieved first of all through memorization by reciters, and by the recording of the entire collection of verses into a highly special and protected book.

What does the Qur'an contain?

Its intention is purely prophetic – to touch the human heart, and to draw each individual to an awareness that there is an eternal scheme of things: that this life and this world that we see and experience are not all there is, and that human beings are not just animals but God's creations, each existing for a purpose.

When the Qur'an is recited, Muslims believe they are hearing Allah Himself speaking to them. Just as the words were given directly to Muhammad, so it often seems that the same words are addressing a person individually – an experience that can and does move many to tears, especially when the words come as an answer to a crisis, or something long worried about.

It is a voice assuring people directly that they are watched over and cared for – the aim is to help people to realize it.

Human lives are not haphazard, although they may be short and often traumatic. They are precious, and the time spent on earth is the learning- and testing-ground for their real existence, the return to God and ultimate future in the Life to Come.

Sudanese boy with verses inscribed on a wooden board.

The Prophet said: 'No people get together to recite the Book of Allah and learn it together among themselves, but peace comes down to them, divine mercy covers them, and angels surround them.' Many Muslims feel blessed from just hearing it recited, even if they do not understand the Arabic. However, if there is no understanding and no beneficial action to follow, then the readers are '*like donkeys, carrying books*' (Surah 62.5), bearing the weight of them but gaining nothing.

The memorized Qur'an

The Qur'an was preserved in thousands of human hearts many years before it was gathered into a book. Arabs had a long tradition of preserving their histories, genealogies and poetry by rote, and since the recitation of passages from the Qur'an was a key part of daily prayer, Muslims were committing it to memory and cross-checking the memories of those reciting even while its revelation proceeded.

A devoted Muslim who has learned the entire Qur'an is known as a *hafiz* (pl. *huffaz*), literally 'a guardian'. They were and are highly respected, and won this title by passing one or more tests, such as being asked to continue the recitation of a passage chosen at random. To this day, if a congregation is at all large, several *huffaz* are bound to be present, and any reciter who stumbles or forgets will soon be corrected.

A person who recites the Qur'an adhering to the proper rules of recitation is known as a *qari'*. They do not have to have memorized the entire Qur'an, although many have done so.

The written Qur'an

Muhammad certainly had literate friends who wrote down verses, and also had scribes to write for him. There was as yet no paper, and since vellum was extremely expensive, they used whatever materials were available – bits of broken pot, large animal bones, white flat stones, dried palm leaves.

Arabic writing of the time was an incomplete script (like ancient Hebrew) – just consonants. It did not include vowels or other signs needed to distinguish between words. For example, in English the letters 'FR' could be 'far', 'for', 'fair', 'fire', etc. In these circumstances, if there were any doubt about a word, the memorized version could actually be a better source than the written one; but then again, there were several regional dialects, so even the spoken word could be open to several interpretations.

The revealed order of the Book

The order in which the verses were placed was also a matter of divine guidance. As the Prophet received each new revelation he was told where it should go in the text revealed so far, and it was included there when the passage was next used in prayer. Each Ramadan the Prophet was called upon to recite the whole collection in the angel's presence, and the finalized text was checked with the angel twice, shortly before the Prophet died.

The first complete written Qur'an

The sections of the Qur'an written down by private individuals were much treasured, but they presented a problem. If unchecked it was possible that they could have been incomplete, or contained mistakes.

must know

Each *surah* is named after some striking incident or word in it, so some have strange names, such as 'al-Baqarah' ('the Cow'), 'al-Ankabut' ('the Spider') and 'al-Maida' ('the Table'). Others have names of Allah – 'al-Nur' ('the Light'), 'al-Rahman' ('the Merciful'). One *surah* is named after Mary, mother of Jesus. The Cow is actually about religious duties, divorce laws and rules governing fair conduct of war, but its title comes from a passage teaching that extremism is misguided and irritating: Moses is pestered by his people for closer and closer definitions of a simple command to sacrifice a cow, making it almost impossible to carry out.

The writer might have inscribed the passage before
all the verses revealed to the Prophet (and later
inserted within those passages) had been revealed,
and so on.

A mere two years after the Prophet's death the
Muslims fought a fierce battle at Yamama in which
many of the *huffaz* were killed. The Prophet's
successor, Abu Bakr, was urged to admit that the
time had come to create a *mushaf* (codex),
presenting all the verses as a complete written
collection on sheets (*suhuf*) that could be fastened
together, so that nothing would be lost. The scribe
Zayd agreed, but reluctantly, since he would be
acting without the Prophet's authorization. Zayd did
not alter the messages in any way, or add explana-
tions or editorial comments, but checked and cross-
checked everything with surviving *huffaz* and
arranged the sheets in the order the Prophet had
specified.

When Abu Bakr died, this precious collection was
passed to Umar, and on his death it was kept by his
daughter Hafsah (one of the Prophet's widows).

Uthman's 'recension'

Of course, followers were still writing down verses,
reciting them in their own dialects, and also possibly
making translations. This brought with it the added
dangers of personal interpretations and misinterpre-
tations creeping in. Twenty years after the Prophet's
death, Caliph Uthman ordered Zayd to preside over a
group of scribes to produce a set of copies of
Hafsah's text in the Quraysh dialect, using the
specially prepared skins of goats sacrificed during

Hajj. When they were completed, Uthman gathered together all the acknowledged experts present in the capital for a public reading, and they verified that this was indeed the authentic text.

He kept one copy for himself and had the others transported to the chief Muslim cities – Makkah, Madinah, Kufa, Damascus, Cairo and Sana' – with the order that any existing private copies should be checked for full agreement against this 'standard' text, and if they deviated, they should be destroyed.

Was Uthman's recension text changed?

Muslims always insist that the Qur'an, as it was completed before the death of the Prophet, has remained unchanged and uncorrupted ever since. Critics of Islam suggest that this is not true, and that changes have been made. There are several reasons why this suggestion is made.

• As Islam spread, it was difficult for Muslims of non-Arab origin to recite the Qur'an correctly without vowels, or marks above or below letters to indicate phonetic value or stress, so these were added *c.* 685–705.

• Some rare manuscripts might have survived the check against Uthman's recension, and might have included incomplete, inaccurate or misplaced texts.

• Some direct words from God were not given as part of the Qur'an – these were known as *hadith qudsi*. It was debated whether some of the prayers revealed to the Prophet were intended to be part of the Qur'an or separate from it. A very few codices omitted some of them, while others included a few extra prayers.

It is unlikely that anyone has ever attempted to alter even a single letter of the Arabic Qur'an for their own personal reasons, since it would be noticed immediately and provoke an outcry.

The content of the Qur'an

The Qur'an does not consist of minutely detailed laws and regulations, but outlines the basic framework for each aspect of human activity – social life, commerce and economics, marriage and inheritance, penal laws and international conduct – by appealing to the mind and heart of each individual who reads it.

The first revelations received by the Prophet are mainly found at the end of the Qur'an. They are short, dramatic outbursts, sometimes cryptic, and

A beautifully inscribed Qur'an.

often contain warnings of dire consequences for those who have rejected belief in God. But although warnings are stern, Allah also reveals Himself as the Guide, the Compassionate One who calls people so that they find forgiveness, motivation and peace.

The longer Madinah *surat*, revealed when the Prophet was actually the ruler of a state, give legislation, and many detailed instructions for every aspect of life. For example, Surah 17.34–7:

• You shall not go near the property of an immature orphan, except with the good intention of improving it.

• You shall fulfil your pledges.

• You shall give full measure when you measure, and weigh with an even scale.

• You shall not follow anyone blindly in matters of which you have no knowledge.

Girls studying the Qur'an.

did you know?

Some commands are very specific: '*If any of you die and leave widows behind, they are allowed to mourn for four months and ten days.*' (Surah 2.234) The length of time for other relatives or friends was only three days – more than that was considered lack of faith.

• You shall not walk arrogantly on the earth, for you can neither rend the earth asunder nor attain the height of the mountains.

Bible 'celebrities'

Over 50 Bible celebrities are important Qur'an celebrities too (including 24 named prophets), usually mentioned because of the moral or spiritual significance of their mission but with few details. It seems to be assumed that readers will already be familiar with their names and stories. However, Muslims do consider material in the Bible to have been edited by fallible scribes and historians, sometimes with personal axes to grind (which was one reason why they believed the Qur'an was necessary). Therefore, anything in the Bible that agrees with the Qur'an is accepted, and anything that disagrees is rejected.

Study and interpretation

Study of the Qur'an is known as *tafsir* (exegesis). A person could delve into it for a lifetime and still find something new every time. On one level, it is very straightforward, and accessible to any person who reads it; at the same time, it contains mysteries and allegories, things that are not to be taken literally but interpreted by scholars and people of spirituality. Any process that depends on the talents of such interpreters, of course, is always open to debate.

For example, the Qur'an cites numerous physical details in its descriptions of the states of being in the Life to Come, yet it also makes clear that the true nature of these states lies beyond the comprehension of the human mind.

A selection of quotes from the Qur'an

'O believers! Stand out firmly for Allah, as witnesses to fair dealing, and let not the hatred of others towards you make you swerve towards wrong and depart from justice. Deal justly, that is next to piety.' (Surah 5.9)

'If you retaliate, then retaliate only to the extent of the wrong done against you; but if you endure with patience, indeed the better reward is with those who endure with patience. So endure with patience, since it is none but Allah who gives you the strength to endure adversity.' (Surah 16.126-8)

'Good and evil are not alike. Repel evil with that which is better, and the one who was your enemy will become your intimate friend.' (Surah 41.35-6)

'Say: O unbelievers! I do not worship that which you worship, nor will you worship that which I worship....To you be your religion, and to me mine.' (Surah 109)

'Those who submit their whole selves to Allah and are doers of good, they will get their reward with their Lord; on such shall be no fear nor shall they grieve.' (Surah 2.112)

'If all the waters of the sea were ink with which to write the words of my Lord, the sea would surely be drained before His words are finished, even if we were to add to it sea upon sea.' (Surah 18.109).

must know

Verses about some well-known biblical characters can be found in the Qur'an:
• Abraham – Surah 15.51-74, 19.41-50, 2.124-130
• Joseph – Surah 12.4-101, 40.34
• Moses – Surah 10.87-90, 7.103-160
• Solomon – Surah 21.78-80, 27.17-44
• Jesus – Surah 19.16-37, 4.171-173, 5.112-117

must know

Muslims treat the Qur'an with enormous respect, and follow a few rules:
• Before reciting, Muslims need to be in the state of *wudu* or ritual cleanliness (see p. 67).
• They should be wearing clean clothes, and be in a clean place.
• Where ritual purity is impossible – for example, women who are menstruating or have recently given birth – the Qur'an should not be touched.
• Muslims adopt a special position for reading the Qur'an (although this is not compulsory) to remind themselves that it is not just an ordinary book. They do not read slumped in a chair. They often sit cross-legged on the floor with the Qur'an on a little wooden 'throne' or *kursi* in front of them.
• The Qur'an should never be placed on the floor, or on a surface where someone might absent-mindedly or in *continues overleaf*

Two things are very important:
• The preservation of the exact words of the text, so that the source of that which is being interpreted always remains unaltered, and available for future scholars to ponder from their position of advanced knowledge and technology.
• The study of the *spirit* of the text, not just the words, in order to arrive at its correct principles and meaning.

The danger of fundamentalism is its almost wilful determination to cling to the letter of the text rather than seeking out its spirit. When this happens, conflict with modernism is bound to arise. See Chapter 10 for more on this topic.

Qur'anic mysteries

Qur'anic mysteries are intriguing.
• Two passages refer to the Qur'an as 'inscribed on an Imperishable (or Preserved) Tablet'. Some commentators take this literally, and believe there is an actual 'heavenly tablet' upon which the Qur'an has been inscribed since all eternity, so that everything is predestined until the Day of Judgement.
• Nineteen *surat* begin with unexplained, isolated letters. The meaning or significance of these 'lonely' letters has baffled scholars right from the start, and although numerous theories have been proposed there is no universally accepted explanation. If the Prophet himself knew their meaning, he never revealed it.
• The 'Code of 19' is a mystery of the computer age, propounded by Dr Rashid Khalifa. Do the numerous coincidences regarding the number 19 in the Qur'an furnish proof that the text was designed in an extra-extraordinary manner by a real Divine Being, kept a

well-guarded secret for 14 centuries, only to be revealed when humans had the technology to investigate the phenomenon? After initial enthusiasm, and many keen disciples, most scholars have now lost interest in his theory. Visit www.19.org/english/articles/code19.htm if you want to know more.

Misinterpretation and distortion of meaning

Much mischief can be caused and injustices done by taking verses or parts of verses out of context, with no regard for the spirit of the text. For example, there are passages (eagerly seized upon by those intent on terrorist activity) where God grants permission to Muslims to slay their enemies – but when one reads the following verses it can be clearly seen that what

ignorance place something on top of it – like a cup of coffee!
• When not in use, it is wrapped in something to keep it free of dust, and usually placed on a high shelf or somewhere special, to show it respect.

Reading the Qur'an on a wooden *kursi*.

did you know?

The skill of the *qari'* in reciting the Qur'an with soul, heart, mind, tongue and body, is known as *tilawah*. The Arabic term for the rules governing how the Qur'an should be read is *tajwid*.

God seeks is forgiveness, peace and mercy. If Muslim scholars are to deduce principles from the Qur'an, they are expected to study not only the text as it is now, but also the chronological order of the verses, the historical background, the context, and the reasons why they were revealed.

Lost in translation?

Although the Qur'an was revealed in the Arabic language and Muslims all over the world recite it in that language, only a small percentage of Muslims in today's world are Arabs, or speak Arabic.

Translations are only as good as the skill of the translators. Should they try to preserve the literal words of the Qur'an, with all their strange idioms, or should they translate a loaded Arabic word with a phrase or sentence that better conveys the meaning in modern terms?

Non-Arabic-speaking Muslims can now find the Qur'an in most of the world's languages, the best versions supplied with footnotes and suggested alternatives. Muslim scholars all aspire to master Arabic, and those with no Arabic usually refer to several translations, of which many can now be found on the Internet.

Superstitious misuse of the Qur'an

Some Muslims use miniature Qur'ans, or tiny scrolls that contain holy texts encased in a piece of jewellery, as charms (*ruqya*), or in a superstitious way – supposedly to protect the wearer. Some will dip a text in water and use it to bathe a wound, or crumble text into water and drink it to promote healing. This was certainly not a practice encouraged by the

Prophet – he taught that the source of all healing and protection is Allah alone, to whom one may pray for healing if it is His will, or to be shown the right way to care for and help the sufferer through their ordeal if their suffering is part of their test of life.

Desecration

Muslims are horrified by desecration of the Qur'an. Even ephemeral literature such as a newspaper that might contain God's name or a quotation from the Qur'an is disposed of carefully. Muslims wearing jewellery bearing the name of God will remove it before entering lavatories or while engaged in sexual intimacy. It is offensive to Muslims to use holy text in disrespectful ways. Nike were forced to apologize and withdraw stock in 1997 after the 'air' logo on their basketball shoes was said to look like the Arabic-script spelling of Allah. No wonder the allegations made in 2005 that guards at the US military base in Guantanamo Bay urinated on the Qur'an and flushed pages down the lavatory in front of Muslim prisoners fuelled widespread controversy and riots.

Qur'ans in public places

The current-day availability of the Qur'an in shops, or for use in schools and libraries, is a matter for concern to the very pious, for they are obviously constantly fingered by all and sundry and not given special status or treatment. However, these books are required for information and study, so many pragmatic Muslims now regard only special Qur'ans in Arabic as ritually sacred, whereas for translations the rules can be somewhat relaxed.

want to know more?

• **Useful translations of the Qur'an in English have been made by Yusuf Ali, Marmaduke Picthall, Abdel Haleem, Aishah Bewley and Rashad Khalifa.**
• **For a strict Wahhabi translation, see M.T al-Hilali and Muhsin Khan.**
• **Two excellent translations with commentaries are those of the Swedish convert Muhammad Asad and Pakistan's Sayyid Abu'l Ala Mawdudi.**

3 What Muslims believe

The faith of Islam is based upon three basic concepts – the real existence of One True God, the Almighty; the real existence of an unknown and unknowable state of existence above and beyond, and before and after, this earthly existence; and the requirement of justice that if our place in that state depends ultimately upon the choices made by our free will to accept or reject the Will of God, then it is His duty to let us know the principles of that Will by sending revelations through His specially chosen messengers, the prophets. This chapter outlines these main teachings of Islam.

What Muslims believe

At some stage, all thinking people ask deep questions – Who am I? Why do I exist? What am I supposed to do with my life? Will my life end with my death? Will I face judgement and a life to come? How can I know anything about all this? If there is a God, how can I know anything about Him?

Page 46: Decorative tile-work, Alhambra, Granada, Spain. Even on a small sample, it is fascinating to pick a line and follow it.

Tawhid – the existence and One-ness of God

The first Muslim belief is *tawhid* – the One-ness of God (from *wahid*, meaning 'one'). God has no partners, no equal, but is totally other, distinct, unique. Human beings believe all sorts of things about all sorts of entities, but Muslims affirm that there is only One God, the Almighty, the Supreme. The word *al-Lah*, or Allah, means 'the Almighty'. All the other beliefs of Islam start from this basic premise – it is the key to the faith, and without genuinely believing this in the depths of one's heart and mind, one cannot be a Muslim. The opposite of *tawhid* is *shirk*, meaning to believe some other thing has power like God's, or that God shares His power with something or someone else, or that anything can have the power to override God's will.

For Muslims, to worship, ask help from, or try to manipulate natural forces, or statues or idols, is not only pointless but also forbidden. To try to take on God's functions oneself is blasphemy – God Alone is the Healer, Judge and Avenger. Muslims believe it is not for them to claim to know who is succeeding or failing in life, or to seek vengeance for wrongs done to them.

The 'Beautiful Names'

In one of the earliest *surat* (Surah 87), the doctrine of *tawhid* was compressed into a single sentence, that Allah's 'name' should be glorified ('hallowed') and exalted. In fact, He revealed a series of names or titles, known as the Beautiful Names, which are actually attributes (Surah 59.22-24).

Most of the Names deal with His loving nature and compassion towards humanity, but some are perhaps surprising to a non-Muslim. God is not only the Merciful, the Provider, the Generous, the Exalter, the Bestower of Honour, the Giver of Life, the Expediter, the Manifest, the Forbearing, the First – He is also the Subduer, the With-holder, the Abaser, the Humiliator, the Causer of Death, the Delayer, the Hidden, the Avenger, the Last. It is interesting to note that not once, in all the 23 years of the revelation to Muhammad, did God ever use the name 'Father' of Himself.

God is First Cause, Creator

Muslims believe that God is the source, origin, cause, creator and maintainer of not only our world and our universe, but also everything that is – most of which lies beyond our knowledge (Surah 6:103). He is First Cause of all the laws that govern its origin and continued existence, its development and destiny.

God is Transcendent, which means He is beyond our understanding, but He is also Immanent, most intimately involved with every aspect of life. He is 'closer' and more vital to each person than their jugular vein (Surah 15.16). He is Omnipotent, which means He has the power to do anything He wills. Nothing else can have power except by His leave.

must know

There are six major articles of belief in Islam:
• belief in God (Allah), the Alone, the Absolute (*tawhid*);
• belief in the angels (*mala'ikah*);
• belief in the Books sent by God (*kutubiyyah*);
• belief in the prophets and messengers sent by God (*risalah*);
• belief in the Day of Judgement (*qiyamah*) and in life after death (*akhirah*);
• belief in destiny or fate (*qadar*).

He is Omniscient, which means He has all knowledge, and is fully aware of everything that happens in the universe, including our private thoughts, motives and intentions. Nothing can be hidden from Him. '*There is not so much as the weight of an atom on the earth or in Heaven that is hidden from your Lord, and not the most microscopic nor the most vast of these things but is recorded in a clear record.*' (Surah 10.61)

It makes no difference to a Muslim whether the world/universe has or does not have a beginning, whether or not there was a Big Bang. In either case, its creation comes from God, whether finite or infinite. Creation was not something that just happened and that was that – the world is transient by nature, always changing and moving, continuously in flux, in a state of being created and recreated. The jury is still out on whether evolution exists or not – if it does, then it is guided evolution.

That which is created not only comes from Him, it is also returning to Him. Muslims believe '*we are Allah's and indeed, to Him we are returning*' (Surah 2.156), and that the end of everything rests with Allah (Surah 79.44, 42.53).

God's relationship with human beings
God created humanity from 'earth', i.e. the physical environment upon which the physical entity of a human body is entirely dependent and inextricably linked through the process of breathing, eating, digesting, etc. God also granted human beings something that was not physical – the *nafs*, or soul, with its capacity for conscious moral awareness, the ability to distinguish between good and evil, freedom

of choice and volition, and the power to act upon choices made. When God withdraws the *nafs* the body will disintegrate back into the environment and the *nafs* must return to God, who will judge each individual on the basis of this lifetime.

Al-ghayb (the unknown)

The matters of *al-ghayb* are transcendent, standing not just beyond our sight or awareness, but beyond our ability to know. God Himself is, of course, totally transcendent. We cannot decide to see Him, or be aware of Him by means of any of our senses. We can only know or be aware of Him if it is His desire. He uses angels to communicate His will and 'presence' to us.

It is not possible for us to know about angels, or the Hereafter, or the spirit or soul. We know we are alive, but we do not know what life is. What matters is whether or not we enter *tasleem* – the state of being aware that there is a Divine Law according to which all those unseen, unknown aspects of life work.

Soul and spirit

Muslims believe that every human being has a *nafs*, the entity that *is* each individual. Our bodies are in constant growth, change and decline – the *nafs* is our permanent *persona*. It is the *nafs* that makes our choices in life, and which will be judged. It vacates the body during sleep, and is taken to the Afterlife following death. (Surah 39.42)

Humans also have access to the *rouh* or spirit, something within them (Surah 17.85), a gift from God that enables humans to make the most of knowledge. It is *not* you, or yours, but all people have access to it as the guide of their conscience, and its

purpose is to enable the soul to make the right
decisions. Animals have *nafs*, but not *rouh* – they
have a life-force, but do not have the ability to
choose to be forgiving, honourable, dishonest or
creative, etc.

Everyone is born innocent, in the state of *fitra*
(meaning 'to bring forth', 'to originate'), with an
innate conscience and awareness through the *rouh*
of the difference between right and wrong, which
develops into a conviction that there is an ideal to be
aspired to, and a purpose for life that involves a
Divine Being.

Self-satisfaction and self-preservation can
frequently lead us to actions that oppose living in
fitra, but if we act against *fitra* (by lying, cheating,
stealing, bullying, betraying our loved ones, etc.),
we feel guilt and shame. These are not matters that
trouble the rest of nature.

Angels
Angels are an order of being created by God to be
His agents, and as such have no free will but always,
automatically, carry out His will. They are 'His
enabling activity' (similar to the Christian concept of
the Holy Spirit). They are made of a substance
(described as 'light') that our eyes cannot see – but
they can make themselves visible, if God wills, in any
shape or form, and people can often feel their
unseen presence. Like God, they do not have gender.

Angels can travel faster than the speed of light – in
effect, instantaneously. There are billions of them,
they can be inconceivably minute or vast (filling the
space between earth and Heaven), of a single cell, a

single leaf, or a continent. They are found everywhere, on every created particle, attending to its created nature and function within the cosmos.

Every person has two 'guardian' angels, the *kiramun katibeen*, who can guard or guide their individual according to God's will, but whose main task is to record the passage of their life, their good and bad deeds and intentions (Surah 50.16-18). This is not to give God information, for He already knows everything. It is to show the deceased, for part of their judgement is to *realize* what they have done or not done, and its consequences.

An angel's role as a guardian or 'protecting friend' (Surah 41.31) does not mean that they are able to protect someone from physical harm (unless God commands it). Importantly, they can act through the *rouh*, by putting thoughts into our minds, and awareness of right and wrong into our consciences.

Jinn

Jinn (from the Arabic word *janna*, to hide or conceal) are a separate order of beings described as being made of 'fire'. They live in a world parallel to ours, and are normally invisible to humans – but they can see us. Unlike angels, they have free will, and can either obey or openly defy God, like humans. The chief *jinn* (the first recorded thing to have disobeyed God), is called Iblis, or Shaytan.

They can be harmless (Surah 72 mentions some *jinn* who accepted Islam), or playful and exasperating, but can also be malign. They may whisper and deceive, cause doubt and insecurity, and lead astray. They can take advantage of moments of human

did you know?

• Jibril (or Gabriel) is God's chief Archangel, the messenger, also called the 'Spirit of God' or 'Holy Spirit'.
• Mika'il (or Michael) is the Archangel of Mercy, bringer of blessings, consolation (including rain), and is a guardian of blessed places.
• Israfil (or Raphael) brings healing, and is the angel who blows the trumpet to inaugurate the Day of Judgement; the first blast destroys everything, and the second blast resurrects all beings to face their future.
• Azra'il is the Angel of Death, responsible for taking souls of humans from their bodies.
• Malik is the Guardian of Hell, along with 19 other angels.
• Ridwan is the Keeper of Paradise.
• Munkar and Nakir are angels who question the dead when they are buried.

weakness, such as when someone is angry, confused or feeling rebellious, when about to perform a challenging religious duty (such as getting up at dawn), or when being tempted to do wrong.

All human beings have at least one *jinn* that 'attaches' itself to them throughout their lives, known as a *qareen*. The Prophet said that even he had one, but he always managed to defeat its evil promptings.

Jinn are also said to have the ability to possess and take over the minds and bodies of other creatures in certain circumstances. Sometimes it seems as if the *jinn* has sexual urges towards or is obsessed by the person it tries to possess, or sometimes it brings an atmosphere of overwhelming melancholy, but most of the time it seems to have malicious intent, as if it enjoyed luring people into confusion, lust, jealousy, rage and self-destruction (or suicide). The Prophet warned people not to attract trouble by involving themselves in or becoming interested in the supernatural, or by loitering in places where *jinn* were likely to feed on our fears and imaginations. Muslims also believe that *jinn* are behind such occult activities as mediumship.

Satan (Shaytan or Iblis)

Satan is the chief *jinn*. Satan's great sins were pride and disobedience – when God told both angels and *jinn* to bow down to (i.e., acknowledge and assist) his newly created humans, Satan refused. After that, there was enmity between Satan and humanity, and he swore to lead astray as many humans as possible.

It is acknowledged that God, as source of everything, is also the source of evil. Satan is allowed to tempt us – by resisting temptation we are raised spiritually and develop our potential.

Risalah (prophecy)

Since Muslims believe that it lies beyond the power of human comprehension to know anything about God at all unless He chooses to reveal it by means of a messenger or apostle, it is perfectly possible to spend an entire lifetime without ever having any awareness of God.

The sending of insight from the World of the Unseen is called *risalah*, or prophecy, and Muslims believe that God has always sent messengers or prophets to people, up until the sending of the Qur'an. The messengers were people to whom God

Muslims praying beside the tomb of the Prophet Hud (Eber) in the Hadhramawt, Yemen.

revealed an intimate knowledge of reality and the true laws of life, and entrusted with the task of bringing humanity back to the original path from which it had strayed.

Muslims accept that the first human being, Adam, was also the first prophet. Jesus is revered as the Messiah, the virgin-born worker of miracles (without the understanding that this made him divine), and one of the greatest of all God's messengers.

The seal of the Prophets

Muhammad, the last Messenger, was entrusted with the same mission as the earlier prophets. He was not called to reveal very much to humanity that was new; on the whole, the message emphasized four issues that the previous prophets had all been called to reveal – the One-ness of God, the goodness and power of God, the moral responsibility of human beings, and the judgement awaiting all people on the Day of Resurrection.

Muslims believe that what was given to Muhammad was the *seal* of all that had gone before. Muslims were expected to '*believe in God, and in the revelation granted to us, and... in all that was given to Moses, Jesus and all the other Messengers from the Lord. We make no distinction between them. To God alone we surrender.*' (Surah 3.84)

Destiny, free will and determinism

'Al-Qadr' is the doctrine of Allah's complete and final control over the fulfilment of events, or destiny. The argument of free will versus determinism is one of the most difficult of all theological problems, as the belief that God knows absolutely everything, including the future, has to be balanced against the notion that human beings have been granted free will to make their own choices in life.

If God knows in advance everything that will happen to a person, then that person's life must be entirely predestined. Many Muslims simply accept just that, and believe that everything that comes to pass was written long before its origins were set in motion, in the heavenly decrees. You often hear the word *maktub* – 'it is written'. This leads to the logical conclusion that if God does not intervene to stop particular courses of action or their outcomes, then He alone is responsible for them, or to blame for them.

However, it is a mistake to assume that Islam is a fatalistic religion. One relevant passage in the Qur'an states: '*Truly, Allah does not change the condition of any people until they first change what is in themselves.*' (Surah 13:11) This certainly indicates that humans can alter their destiny. Fatalism is a misunderstanding of the entire system of God's sending messengers to humanity.

The whole point of *risalah* is that humans are expected to listen and then make choices, and adjust their lives accordingly (Surah 6:91; 23:73). Even the most wicked are capable of reform. That is why the prophets were entrusted with the task of giving spiritual counsel to *everyone* – so that they may awaken their human conscience and that God may forgive them.

The most satisfactory conclusion is that an Omniscient God does indeed know everything and every possibility, but He does not think, as humans do, in a 'straight line'. He must know *all* the possible

must know

There is no teaching in the Qur'an that when Muslim men die they will be able to have all their sexual urges gratified by beautiful dark-eyed virgins, or that martyrs will be rewarded with 72 virgins (as is often mistakenly claimed in the Western media when they report on suicide bombings).

outcomes of *all* the billions of choices simultaneously, while genuinely not influencing the fall of the dice.

Akhirah (eternal life)

The nature of our Afterlife and our relationships in it are part of *al-ghayb* (the unknown). People throughout the ages have indulged in all sorts of speculation about the delights of the rewards of the good and the horrors of the punishments of the wicked. About a quarter of the Qur'an is dedicated to this subject.

'*Think not of those who are slain in the way of Allah as dead. Nay, they are living. They have provision with their Lord, and are in bliss.*' (Surah 3.169)

Death (*mawt*) proves the transitory nature of earthly existence – even if people deny the existence of God they cannot deny death. However, Muslims believe that after their earthly lives have finished they do not cease to exist, but enter a new state of existence known as *akhirah*, or the Afterlife. Our journey in the direction of *akhirah* is actually a return to our original home, after a temporary time away.

After death souls enter the state of *barzakh*, a period of waiting until the Day of Judgement, or Day of Resurrection, when they will be reunited with newly created bodies and will go to their future state of existence, either Heaven (*Jannah* or Paradise) or Hell (*Jahannam*).

Azra'il, the Angel of Death, is responsible for parting souls from their bodies, the actual process depending on their record of good or bad deeds. For those who lived badly, the soul is ripped out very painfully. For the righteous, their souls slide peacefully like a 'drop of water dripping from glass'. Immediately after death, the souls face two angelic questioners regarding their faith.

The soul was that which caused a person's body to function as one living entity, and once the soul is withdrawn bodies revert to their millions of component parts and disintegrate back into 'earth'. Meanwhile, the soul enters a period of waiting, the length of which may be centuries in earth time, but will pass without any sense of time for the 'dead'. Whether the body has been burnt, drowned or eaten by scavengers has no influence on the recreated body, resurrected at the time when God wills and God only knows.

People's experiences in the state of *barzakh* will also be very different. Those who lived good lives will be able to travel in soul-state for enormous distances, having all sorts of pleasant and enlightening experiences – but those who were bad will be shut in and confined to the grave. The Prophet warned people that the punishment of the grave was like being crushed and buried alive.

On the Day of Judgement, or Day of Resurrection (*Yawm al-Qiyamah*), Israfil will sound the trumpet, the 'graves will be opened', and souls will be given new bodies – not earth bodies, but an entirely new creation in forms beyond our present capacity for understanding (Surah 56:60-61). During their lives on earth everyone had free will to believe or not in the reality of God and the life to come – but once they are awakened actually *in* their future state, whether they like it or not, they will be obliged to face up to the *significance* of everything they did, and how their actions affected others (Surah 23:99-100). None will be able to protest – they will all see their own records in the books recorded by their angels (Surah 17:13-14).

Muslims are confident that their judgement will be absolutely fair – and that no person will be able to excuse another or buy another off, or be made to suffer for the sins of anyone else (Surah 35.18).

After this comes the future state of existence, either Heaven (*Jannah*, or Paradise) or Hell (*Jahannam*). The judged will either pass over the Bridge, *al-Sirat*, 'finer than a hair and sharper than a sword', in complete confidence, or else slip into the abyss. Beyond the Bridge lies the *Hawzu'l Kawthar* ('Lake of

Abundance'), where the Prophet said he would be
found waiting for his friends.

The Qur'an is full of detailed descriptions of
beautiful gardens with rivers running through them,
people enjoying peace and contentment (including
delicious foods and wine that gives no hangover!),
and the company of loved spouses made young
again, plus other companions of a different order of
being altogether, called *huri*. Similarly, there are
horrendous descriptions of the punishments
suffered by those doomed to Hell – scorching fires,
thorns and thistles for food, and scalding drinks.
However, most Muslim scholars feel that these
descriptions should be interpreted symbolically –
since we have specifically been told that these
matters lie beyond our capacity to understand
(Surah 32.17).

The biggest problem for those who believe that
God is compassionate is the fact that a Hell exists at
all, and that anyone might end up in that state. Islam
has produced plenty of preachers who have very
wrongly 'encouraged' people to believe in God
through *fear*. Less stern counsellors may deny the
concept of Hell altogether, believing that God would
destroy no one. Many well-meaning graveside
comforters encourage mourners to believe that this
must be so.

However, Muhammad taught the existence of
Hell, and pointed out to one group of mourners who
were highly confident that his beloved friend would
certainly be rewarded by Allah, that he had no right
to assume this – only God knew the secrets of our
lives and could judge fairly. Happily, many sinners do
not end up in Hell because they repent and are

genuinely sorry, and turn to God for forgiveness before the end of their lives.

Are Heaven and Hell eternal states? We do not know. Most Muslims accept that these states are final, but not all scholars agree. One passage in the Qur'an teaches that *'those who are wretched shall be in the Fire... They will dwell there for all the time that the heavens and earth endure, **unless your Lord wills otherwise**....And those who are blessed shall be in the Garden, where they will dwell for all the time that the heavens and the earth endure, **unless your Lord wills otherwise** – a gift unceasing.'* (Surah 11.106-108)

Will we stay married in Heaven, or will our relationship really only be 'till death us do part'? One *hadith* described *huris* rebuking wives who distressed their husbands, pointing out they were just their guests for the duration of their marriages, after which they would return to their loved ones in Paradise. What happens in cases of polygamy, or where people have married more than once in their lifetimes, perhaps because of death or divorce?

Islam teaches that in the life to come we will be resurrected in forms we know not of – our mode of living is beyond our present comprehension. It may be that such things as eating, drinking and sexual intimacy will not exist, certainly not in the ways that we now recognize them. The Qur'an does suggest, however, that we will be in the company of those we have loved, and continue to love.

want to know more?

• J. Esposito, *Islam, the Straight Path*, Oxford, 2004
• Ismail al-Faruqi, *Islam*, Amana Publications, 2000
• R. Maqsood, *After Death, Life*, Goodword, New Delhi, 1998

4 What Muslims do

The whole aim of Muslim life is *ibadah* (service
to God) by following the Straight Path, bringing
every thought, word and action under control
by conscious choice. A Muslim's every action is
taken for His sake, whether at work, play,
school, or within the home, and is a form of
worship. There are also five compulsory ritual
duties that have to be carried out, known as
the 'Pillars of Islam' – bearing witness, prayer,
purifying their wealth, fasting and making the
pilgrimage to Makkah. This chapter explains
what these entail.

What Muslims do

Muslim worship (*ibadah*) is not just a matter of praying to and praising God. It involves every action of life carried out with the deliberate intention of pleasing Him. Over and above this duty of love, there are five things that Muslims have been asked to do by God, often referred to as the 'Five Pillars of Islam' or *arkan*.

must know

The *qiblah* is the direction of Makkah, faced during prayer. Having a focal point for prayer consolidates the religious feelings of Muslims around the world. In the spiritual sense, the true *qiblah* means to turn the heart in the direction of God – and He, of course, has no fixed location.

Bearing witness

The Shahadah (from the verb *shahida*, 'to testify') is a very simple creed, and is the starting point for Muslim life. '*Ash-hadu an la ilaha ilallah, wa ash-hadu an Muhammad ar-rasul Allah*' means 'I bear witness that there is no God but the Almighty (*Al-Lah*); and I bear witness that Muhammad is the Prophet of Allah.' It is a statement Muslims make daily, and is the foundation for all other beliefs and practices in Islam. However, before the declaration must come belief – simply reciting the words is meaningless.

Ideally, these are the first words a newborn will hear. Children are taught it as soon as they are able to understand it, and Muslims hope to be able to recite it as their last words, or to hear it recited for them. Those wishing to show their conversion to Islam are required to recite it publicly, before two witnesses. The Shahadah is also used for the call to prayer (the *adhan*) five times a day. If the mosque has a tower, a man known as a *muezzin* or *mu'adhin* climbs up and calls aloud:
- *Allahu Akbar!* (four times) God is the Most Great!
- *Ash-hadu an la ilaha illallah* (twice) I bear witness that there is no God but Allah.

Page 62: Detail from the Alhambra, Granada.

• *Ash-hadu an Muhammad ar-rasul Allah* (twice)
I bear witness that Muhammad is the Prophet of
Allah.
• *Hayya al as-salah* (twice) Come to prayer!
• *Hayya al al-falah* (twice) Come to success [or
salvation]!
• *Allahu Akbar* (twice) God is the Most Great!
• *La ilaha illallah* (once) There is no God but Allah!
At the end of the first prayer of the day the phrase 'It
is better to pray than to sleep!' is added – '*as-salatul
khairum min an-naum*'.

The *adhan* gives Muslims time to get ready if they
are going to pray at the mosque. Just before the
actual start of the prayers, a second call to prayer, the
iqamah, is uttered before the congregation. It is the
same as the *adhan*, except that the words '*qad
qamatis salah*' – 'The prayer has begun' – are added
before the final Allahu Akbars.

There is a longer statement of belief which brings
in all the doctrines and practices of Islam: '*It is not
righteousness to turn your faces towards east or west;
but this is righteousness – to believe in God, and the
Day of Judgement, and the angels, and the Book
(meaning all God's genuine revelations to all of His
prophets), and the Messengers; to give from your wealth
out of love for God to your family, to those without
family, to those in need, to the wayfarer (including the
refugee), and to those who ask, and for the setting free
of slaves; to be steadfast in prayer and to practice
regular giving; to fulfil all the promises which you have
made; to be firm and patient in pain and suffering or
any other adversity, and through all periods of panic.
Such are the people of truth, the God-fearing.*' (Surah
2:177)

Mosques are often full for Friday prayers. Outside, those who can't get in may use individual prayer-mats.

The complete way of life and belief of a Muslim is known as the *din* (pronounced 'deen'). It consists of two aspects – *iman* (faith, belief) and *amal* (putting beliefs into action). Muslims who have complete submission and faith established in their hearts are known as Mu'min (from '*iman*').

Prayer (*salah*)

Muslims have two sorts of prayer: their five special compulsory prayers (the *salat*), and the more personal kind (*du'a*). *Salah* is the ritual of move-ments and words (each full sequence of which is called a *rakah*), in which lines of Muslims perform various actions – standing, bending and bowing from the waist, kneeling, and prostrating with their foreheads touching the floor. Muslims are requested by God to perform this ritual prayer five times every day, at specified times.

The discipline of Muslim prayer is intended to purify the heart and bring about spiritual and moral growth. A day punctuated by so many 'meetings' with God brings a deep feeling of closeness and intimacy, peace and tranquillity. Praying with others also encourages equality, unity and brotherhood and helps to develop gratitude and humility. It trains individuals in cleanliness, purity and punctuality, helps to develop discipline and will-power, draws the mind away from personal worries, calms passions and masters baser instincts.

Preparation for prayer

Salah requires a state of ritual purity, which first involves preparing the mind by declaring one's intention (*niyyah*) to come before God. This is to close the mind to all worldly distractions. Secondly, the body is prepared with a special ritual wash known as *wudu* (also pronounced '*wudhu*' or '*wuzu*'). Muslims should also wear clean clothes, and pray in a clean place. In Muslim countries, if forced to pray by the roadside, there are usually little areas set aside for prayer, and Muslims often carry their own prayer-mats.

The *wudu*

There is a difference between everyday washing (*taharah*) and purification for prayer. The routine, as the Prophet taught it, is detailed: 'Wash your hands up to the wrists three times; rinse your mouth three times with water thrown into your mouth with the right hand; sniff the water into the nostrils and blow it out three times; wash the entire face, including the forehead, three times; wipe the top of the head once with the inner surface of both hands together; wash your ears with your forefingers and wipe the back of the ears with your thumbs, and wipe the back of your neck once; wash the right foot and then the left foot up to the ankles three times; let the water run from your hands up to your elbows three times.'

Wudu is always done in a quiet, prayerful manner, for it is in itself part of the act of worship. While washing, Muslims pray that they will be purified from the sins they have committed by hand or mouth, that they will be empowered to do good and refrain from evil.

If water is not available, the worshipper can perform a dry 'wash' known as *tayammum*, which simply involves touching some earth and wiping it over the face, hands and arms in an imitation wash.

Performing *wudu*, Morocco.

must know

Muslims do not have to make a fresh *wudu* before every prayer if they have not 'broken the state' – it is broken by sexual intercourse, discharge leaving the body (such as blood, seminal fluid, urine, faeces, or wind), or if the person has fallen asleep or lost consciousness in some way. Women who are menstruating, or are in the days after childbirth, cannot enter *wudu* and are therefore excused from *salah* prayer. A full bath, known as *ghusl*, is necessary after sexual intercourse, when menstruation has finished, and after contact with dead bodies.

Muslims remove their shoes, and usually pray barefoot. If socks, stockings or tights are worn, it is not considered compulsory to take them off and wash the feet for each prayer so long as Muslims are in *wudu* when they first put them on. Muslims may simply wipe over the socks with wet hands the next time (although many Muslims regard this as laziness).

Men must be covered at least from waist to knee, and women must completely cover themselves, leaving only face and hands visible, and should not be wearing perfume. Sometimes they put on a special prayer outfit. It is not compulsory for men to cover their heads, but many wear a special prayer-cap.

Imams

There are no priests in Islam – each Muslim faces God on a one-to-one basis. Prayers are led by a volunteer, the imam, who must be respected, have good knowledge of Muslim faith, and who knows enough of the Qur'an to recite during prayer. Most mosques have a regular imam these days, but any Muslim may lead the prayer in his absence.

Prayer times

If Muslims are keeping the prayer times properly, their first prayer (the *fajr* – a prayer of two *rakat*) will be before sunrise. It is sometimes called the 'dawn' prayer, but those not used to early hours may not realize that there is quite a long period of time between dawn ('first light') and sunrise. If Muslims oversleep, they are encouraged to pray as soon as possible.

A young Bosnian imam leads some women in prayer.

The other four daily prayers are:
* *Zuhr* (just after the height of the midday sun – four *rakat*)
* *Asr* (during the afternoon, when the shadows have lengthened – four *rakat*)
* *Maghrib* (just after sunset – three *rakat*), and
* *Isha* (in the night – four *rakat*).

Prayers are forbidden at the exact times of sunrise, midday and sunset because of their association with sun worship.

Since the times of sunrise and sunset differ regionally, there are set timetables for congregational prayers at the mosque. Many mosques set up clock faces showing these times, five for the daily prayers and one for the special Friday prayer. The *tahajjud* prayer is an optional prayer performed during the night. It can be performed any time between *isha* and *fajr*.

The Prayer sequence

There are eight acts of devotion in each *rakah*. The first is *takbir*, or glorification, the deliberate shutting out of the world and its distractions. Muslims stand to attention facing the *qiblah*, raise their hands to shoulder-level, and acknowledge the majesty of God, saying 'Allahu Akbar'. The second is to place the right hand over the left on the chest, to praise God and acknowledge His Oneness, to seek shelter from Satan, and to recite Surah 'al-Fatihah'.

Next, another passage from the Qur'an is recited, the choice of the prayer-leader. It can be long or short, but the Prophet recommended keeping public prayers short for those in the congregation suffering

must know

Surah 'al-Fatihah' is the key Muslim prayer. Its translation is: '*In the name of Allah, the Compassionate, the Merciful. All praise be to Allah, the Lord of the Universes, the Most Merciful, the Most Kind, Master of the Day of Judgement. You alone do we worship, and from You alone do we seek help. Show us the straight path, the way of those on whom You have bestowed Your grace, not (the path) of those earning Your anger, those who are going astray.'*

discomfort, coping with children, etc.; the length of private prayers is up to the individual.

The third stage is *ruku*, the bowing. Men place their hands on their knees and bow right over with a straight back; women do not bow quite so deeply. They repeat three times: '*Glory be to my Great Lord, and praise be to Him.*'

Next comes *qiyam*, when Muslims stand up again and acknowledge their awareness of the presence of God with the words: '*God always hears those who praise Him. O God, all praise be to You, O God greater than all else.*'

The humblest of all positions is the *sujud*, or *sajda*. Muslims kneel and touch the ground with their palms, forehead, nose, knees and toes. Their fingers face *qiblah*, and their elbows are raised and not lying on the ground. They repeat three times: '*Glory be to my Lord, the Most High. God is greater than all else.*' Then they kneel up again in a sitting position known as *julus*, palms resting on the knees in a moment of silent prayer, before repeating *sujud* and *julus* again.

At the end of the compulsory sequence they pray for all the brotherhood of the faithful, the congregation gathered there, and for the forgiveness of sins. When they pray for forgiveness, they place their right fist on their right knee and extend the forefinger.

The last action is to turn the head to right and left with the words: '*Asalaam aleikum wa rahmatullah*' – 'Peace be with you, and the mercy of Allah.' This is known as the '*salaam*', and acknowledges not only the other worshippers, but also the attendant guardian angels.

Muhammad made it clear that all prayers valid as *salat* had to fall within the set periods of the day. He also said it was preferable for Muslims to pray together. It was normal practice at that time for women to go to the mosque, and form prayer lines behind those of the men, but some mosques have discouraged the inclusion of women because of cultural beliefs.

Individual prayers

When you see Muslims praying 'out of time' with the congregation, this is because they are praying extra non-compulsory *rakat* or *nafl* prayers, following the practice of the Prophet. It is also normal to pray two *rakat* upon entering a mosque, before the congregation is ready. You always know when the compulsory prayer is to start because someone will call the *iqamah* and everyone will line up behind a leader. When Muslims join the prayer-lines late, they usually make up the missed part after the main prayer is finished. Many Muslims finish the set prayer, then change their position to indicate this, and then pray as many more *rakat* as they like.

Tasbih

Sometimes worshippers carry a string of 33 or 99 beads, and pray quietly while passing the beads through their fingers. These beads are called *tasbih* (or *subhah*). They are divided into three sections by larger beads. The Muslims say '*Subhanallah*' ('Glory be to Allah'), '*Alhamdu lillah*' ('Thanks be to Allah'), and '*Allahu akbar*' ('God is Most Great') 33 times, as they pass the beads.

Friday prayers

Only one prayer in the mosque is compulsory, the midday prayer on Fridays – *salat al-jama'ah*, also known as *salat al-jumah*. During this special prayer of only two *rakat*, which takes the place of the normal *zuhur*, the imam will give two sermons (or *khutbahs*) from the pulpit or *minbar*.

Du'at (personal prayers)

Du'a prayer, which is not formal, does not require *wudu* and can be said anywhere, at any time, is the general awareness of the presence of God throughout the day. It includes private petitions for help, healing, forgiveness or answers to problems, and thanksgiving for blessings and mercies received.

Fasting

Fasting had long been practised by Jews and
Christians, notably on the Day of Atonement for
Jews, and during the period before Easter, known as
Lent, for Christians. The Arabic lunar month of
Ramadan was already a special month of prayer for
the Prophet, but in Islam it became a fast for the
entire month. Muslim fasting means abstaining
from food or drink from first light of dawn until
sunset, and to suspend all sexual intimacy during
those hours.

Ramadan is not only a month of self-discipline and
prayer, but also of peace and compassion. Any
forbidden conduct – such as lying, theft or physical
abuse – would also break the fast as much as eating
food. 'If you do not give up telling lies,' said the
Prophet, 'then God will have no need of your giving
up food and drink in fasting.'

As the fast starts at dawn, most Muslims get up
well before then to eat and drink something
nourishing (a meal known as the *suhur*). Some
families virtually swap day for night, working and
being busy all night, and taking it easy during the
fast of the day. Fasting ends just after sunset.
Muslims usually take a sweet drink or some fruit
before performing the evening prayer. After that,
they may eat normally. When the new moon is
sighted at the end of the Ramadan month, Muslims
celebrate with the Feast of Breakfast – 'Eid ul-Fitr'
(see p. 83).

Some Muslims do not even brush their teeth or
shower, in case they accidentally swallow water.
Some do not even swallow their own saliva but use a
tissue to dispose of it – regarded as unnecessary

piety by scholars who point out that the saliva is already in the body. Some will refuse to take medicine or have injections, although if they become ill they are excused the fast anyway. Diabetics, for example, are issued with warnings to be very careful.

Special practices

During Ramadan there are special prayers held in the mosques every evening called *tarawih* (breaks, or pauses). These divide the recitation of the Qur'an by a *hafiz* (see p. 34) throughout the 30 days, so that the entire text is read through.

Laylat ul-Qadr (see p. 91) is usually celebrated on the 27th Ramadan. Many Muslims spend the whole night in prayer at the mosque. Some Muslims even 'withdraw from the world' (*i'tikaf*) for the last 10 days of Ramadan. Men may stay in the mosque, but women retreat from their normal lives and withdraw to a private room at home. Both are supplied by their families, who also take over their duties.

Zakah – the religious tax

The fourth pillar of Islam is *zakah*, from a word meaning 'to cleanse, be wholesome, purify'.

Muslims acknowledge that Allah is the real owner, and they merely the trustees, of wealth. All of earth's commodities, including cash, should be in use, or in flow. Hoarding is a selfish misuse of a commodity, depriving others who might be able to put it to use. Paying *zakah* therefore allows wealth to circulate more fairly in society, and by paying it Muslims purify themselves and their possessions.

After their duties have been taken care of, Muslims should give up a fortieth (or 2.5 per cent) of their

must know

If food or drink is swallowed by accident or absent-mindedness, this does not break the fast if the slip was genuine. It is also forbidden for Muslims to smoke during the fast, and many use it as a good opportunity to kick the habit.

surplus money, capital or goods to God's service, asking neither recompense nor thanks (Surah 26:109). This 'tax' comes after the savings or excess wealth has been owned for one year, once it exceeds a minimum level known as the *nisab* – the amount considered adequate for the essential needs of the individual or family.

There are eight specific categories of people who should be helped by this giving: the poor; those in great need; those employed to administer the funds; those whose hearts have been recently turned to Islam who are in need; those in bondage and slavery; those in debt; the refugee or traveller in need; and for other specific causes for God's sake.

Muslims normally give anonymously so as not to cause embarrassment. Giving is only done with publicity if it would encourage others to give also (see Surah 2:271).

Paying *zakah* is very much a test of sincerity, as well as unselfishness. There is no authority regulating payment; it is left entirely up to the conscience of the individual. It is not even a state tax in Muslim societies, although the authorities will collect and distribute moneys when required. Being willing to pay it shows that your heart is clean of the love of money and the desire to cling to it.

The Hajj

The Hajj (which means 'to set out with a definite purpose') is the religious high point of a Muslim's life and an event that every Muslim dreams of undertaking. It is the pilgrimage to Makkah, compulsory for every adult Muslim who can afford it, and who is able to go, once in a lifetime. '*It is the*

*duty of all believers towards God to come to the House a
pilgrim, if able to make their way there.'* (Surah 3:91).
Each individual Muslim goes as the 'guest' of God, in
response to His personal request of them to come.
It takes place at a specific time in the Muslim
calendar, in the month of Dhul Hijjah, 70 days after
Ramadan. These days, around 2 million make the
trip each year.

Making the Hajj used to be a considerable sacrifice
and effort, some people travelling for months and
even years overland to reach Makkah. These days,
religious tour guide companies (*mutawwifs*) are
responsible for looking after the Hajjis in their care
from the time they leave home until they return home
again. Some Muslims make the Hajj many times, but
this is not encouraged because the vast numbers
cause considerable difficulties. In fact, anyone who
wishes to make their pilgrimage more than once is
urged to go at the time of a 'Lesser Pilgrimage' (*umrah*).

Sometimes people save for a lifetime to make
the trip, but when at last they have enough money,
they are too old or infirm to go. They may then pay
for someone to go in their place, or donate the
money to charity, knowing that God accepts the
niyyah (intention) of their Hajj, just as if they had
done it. Muslims are also excused if they cannot
afford to go, or if it would cause hardship to their
dependants.

Rules for pilgrims

Pilgrims have to be Muslim (it is not a tourist
attraction), of sound mind, and able to understand
the religious significance of the experience. Children
may be taken along, but it does not count as their

must know

The Saudi Arabian
government allocates
millions of dollars a year
to the Ministry of
Pilgrimage, and the Hajj
Airport at Jiddah is the
largest airport in the
world.

Pilgrims arriving in any way they can.

own Hajj. Pilgrims should be fit enough to cope with the strenuous conditions, although those who leave for Hajj do so knowing they may never return. Many people do pass away while on Hajj, through accident, sickness or old age.

Makkah is regarded by Muslims as a specially holy place, and no non-Muslim is allowed to enter it. It is *haram*, which means both 'sacred' and 'forbidden'. When travellers come to Makkah by road, they will arrive at *miqat* – places where their passports will be checked, to make sure that they are genuine Muslim pilgrims.

Events concerning three prophets are celebrated during the Hajj – the forgiveness and reunion of Adam and Eve; Ibrahim's readiness to sacrifice his son Isma'il (not Isaac, as in the Bible); and the life of obedience of Muhammad.

When Adam and Eve gave in to the temptation of Satan not only did they lose God, they also lost each other. But God watched over them, waiting for the moment when they turned back to Him and exchanged their defiance for the desire for forgiveness. Then He forgave them, and they were reunited on the plain of Arafat, where there is a small hill known as Jabal ar-Rahman, the Mount of Mercy. Muslims believe that it was after this that they built the first shrine dedicated to God on earth, the Ka'bah sanctuary. This is now the most sacred shrine of Islam, the *qiblah* towards which all Muslims turn in prayer five times per day.

The story of Ibrahim differs from that presented in the Bible (in Genesis 22:1–14), for he was not *ordered* by God to sacrifice his son Isma'il, but *dreamed* that this was what God wanted (Surah 37.102). The family was further tested by Satan, who tried to dissuade them from fulfilling God's will, but they repelled him with stones. At the last moment, God intervened and stopped the sacrifice, and a ram was sacrificed instead – the origin of the sacrifice of Eid ul-Adha at the end of Hajj (Surah 37:105).

Later, Ibrahim left Isma'il and his mother Hajarah to God's care beside the Ka'bah, but although they were on a trade route no water-carrying caravans came by. Hajarah ran back and forth seven times between the two hills of Safa and Marwah, desperately seeking help, but when Isma'il was on the point of death Jibril appeared and opened a spring at Isma'il's feet – the spring now called Zamzam.

Later the family was reunited and Ibrahim and Isma'il together rebuilt the sanctuary now known as the Ka'bah. For the last 4000 years or so the Ka'bah has always been reconstructed on the same

must know

The word Ka'bah (from the Arabic, '*muka'ab*') means 'cube' – it is a simple, cube-shaped building, some 13 metres (43 feet) high, built of granite from the surrounding hills. In the eastern corner is set the *Rukn-al-Aswad* (or *al-Hajaru l-Aswad* – the Black Stone), generally thought to be a meteorite. The Ka'bah is covered by a black velvet curtain decorated with gold-embroidered calligraphy (see a picture of this on p. 176).

The spring of Zamzam still flows, in a chamber under the courtyard, and steps lead down to it. Pilgrims drink the water, and collect it in bottles. Some dip their *ihram* cloths in the water and keep them for use later, as their shrouds. The water-providers (*zamzamis*) these days store the water well in advance, replenish containers and paper cups in numerous, strategically located places around the mosque, and continuously refill them as needed. A charitable foundation also bottles Zamzam water for sale throughout the world.

foundations, and the faithful have always gone there on pilgrimage.

The rites of Hajj

It is compulsory for each pilgrim to do four things on Hajj. They must enter the state of *ihram* and put on *ihram* clothing; process around the Ka'bah seven times (the *tawaf*); make the stand at Mount Arafat (the *wuquf*); and circle the Ka'bah again, after returning from Arafat. When pilgrims have completed these four things, they may take the title *hajji* (or *hajjah*).

Separated from the world

To be in *ihram* means to be personally in *haram*, or separated from the world, a special state of holiness. Muslims must strive to keep their minds at peace, and turn them completely to the will of Allah.

First, they take a full bath to purify the body, then their identity begins to slip away as their normal garments are set aside and they enter the state of *ihram*. It becomes obligatory to change into the *ihram* garments at the *miqat* (around 4 kilometres from the Ka'bah shrine). These days many pilgrims put on *ihram* even before they board their planes.

The object of *ihram* garments is purity and equality, single-mindedness and self-sacrifice. Men may only cover themselves with two simple pieces of unsewn white cloth, one wrapped round their waist which reaches to their ankles, and one thrown over the left shoulder – nothing else. Women may wear any plain, loose, full-length clothing and a head veil, so that every part of them is covered except the face, hands and feet. Even if they normally wear a face-veil, they must not do so in *ihram*. They do not have to wear white, although many do.

Once Muslims have put on *ihram* they are totally dedicated to Allah. Normal marital relations are set aside, and anyone who gets engaged, or marries, on Hajj invalidates their pilgrimage.

Men must not wear any jewellery and women may wear wedding rings only. Perfume and scented soap are forbidden. Men must leave their heads uncovered, to express their humility, but they are allowed to carry umbrellas as protection from the sun. Everyone must go barefoot or in sandals that leave the toes and heels bare. They must not cut hair or fingernails, kill any living things (except fleas, bedbugs, snakes and scorpions), or damage plants.

On arrival at Makkah, Muslims start reciting the *talbiyah* prayer, a deeply moving experience as each individual among some 2 million pilgrims cries to Allah that he or she has arrived, in His service.

The *tawaf* is the circling of the Ka'bah seven times in an anticlockwise direction, the first three circuits at a run, if possible. They do this, no matter what time of day or night they arrive. Invalids and the elderly are carried on specially constructed stretcher-chairs. If they can reach the Black Stone they will touch or kiss it – as something the Prophet himself touched – or raise their hands in salute if they cannot get near. The deep hollow in the middle is where it has been worn away by the touch of millions of pilgrims. It is not, however, an object to be worshipped. The crush can be so great, and people so close together, that they can sometimes move without using their feet, swept along in the flow of bodies. At the end of the *tawaf*, they go to the Station of Ibrahim to pray two *rakat*.

did you know?

In the courtyard of the Ka'bah mosque is a stone known as the 'Maqam Ibrahim', which marks the spot where Ibrahim stood to direct building operations. The semi-circular enclosure in front of the Ka'bah marks the traditional site of the graves of Hajarah and Isma'il.

The stand at Mount Arafat.

The Kiswah, the black veil covering the Ka'bah which is lifted during the Hajj, is traditionally made each year in Cairo by male embroiderers. Verses from the Qur'an are embroidered around it, in gold thread. At the end of Hajj it is taken down and cut up into small pieces, given as souvenirs or gifts to selected pilgrims. Pieces are sent to mosques throughout the world, and many Muslims frame their piece and hang it on the wall.

The present door of the Kab'ah (raised 2.25 metres above flash-flood level) is made of solid gold, and is 3.10 metres high, 2 metres wide and about 50 centimetres thick (see picture on page 176). A flight of steps is rolled into position for people to enter the Ka'bah. They rarely do, but there is a ceremony of cleansing before Ramadan and again before Hajj. Inside, the walls are decorated simply, with texts from the Qur'an.

The Sa'i is the memorial of Hajarah's running between the two small hills (now an enclosed passageway). It symbolizes the soul's desperate search for that which gives true life.

On the 8th Dhu'l Hijjah, the pilgrims proceed to the valley of Mina, some 10 km away. This used to be a walk into the desert, but now the town of Makkah reaches virtually as far as the vast 'city' of thousands of identical tents (some sleeping-places are for up to 50 people). Those who cannot afford a tent camp by the roadside. Some pilgrims now miss out Mina and take modern transport straight to Arafat, because of the sheer numbers involved.

On the ninth day, all the pilgrims have to reach the plain of Arafat (24 kilometres east of Makkah) and make their stand before God on or surrounding the

Mount of Mercy, between noon and dusk. If they do not arrive for the standing by sunset, their Hajj is not considered valid.

The pilgrims stand in the sweltering heat for several hours, praying for God's cleansing. It is a time of great mystical and emotional power, and there is a tremendous sense of release – being totally wrapped in love, totally 'washed'. It is a powerful spectacle to see them perform the *zuhr* and *asr* prayers here, especially the moments of prostration and total silence as they bow before Allah.

As the sun disappears over the horizon, the pilgrims start the *nafrah*, the surge back to Makkah. They travel by bus, car, truck, and, as an act of piety, by foot. They stop at Muzdalifah, between Arafat and Mina, where they say the *maghrib* and *isha* prayers, but because of the great crowds, only the earliest to depart arrive in time for *maghrib*, so many make this prayer before leaving. They collect seven small pebbles, and carry them to Mina, arriving by the morning of the 10th Dhu'l Hijjah.

At Mina, there are three huge obelisks, known as *jamrat*, set up to represent Satan, and the pilgrims carry out the *Rajm*, or ritual of casting their pebbles

must know

The *Rajm*, in which pilgrims throw stones at the devil, can be dangerous, as every pilgrim wants to get close enough to 'hurl at the devil' personally. Despite recent improvements and precautions over 350 pilgrims were crushed to death there in the Hajj of 2006. A new approach-way is planned which will ultimately reach 10 levels. Some scholars feel it would be better if this ritual of stoning were only symbolic.

Above: Collecting pebbles.
Below: Pilgrims stoning the tip of the symbol of Satan.

Previous pages:
The Kab'ah shrine-
during the Hajj,
with all three
storeys and
surrounding roads
full of pilgrims .

at them in remembrance of Ibrahim and his family driving away the devil.

On the 10th Dhu'l Hijjah, the pilgrims buy a sheep, goat or young camel, to make their sacrifice and commence the festival of Eid ul Adha, commemorating Ibrahim's willingness to offer his son's life. The meat is then shared out, the excess frozen for distribution, and the rest roasted and eaten. Hajjis may now pay a cash equivalent, purchase a sheep from an Islamic bank to be sacrificed in accordance with Islamic practice, with the meat then distributed to the poor throughout the Muslim world.

At the same time, Muslims all over the world keep unity by buying their own slaughtered animal for the Feast. A complete sheep fills three carrier bags. Some is used, some frozen, and a third must be given away to those too poor to buy their own animal. The sacrificed animals, called *udhiya* or *qurbani*, have to be at least a year old, and good quality.

Once back in Makkah pilgrims make the final *tawaf*, at which point their pilgrimage is complete. After this, men either shave their heads or cut their hair, and women cut off an inch or so of their hair, and wear normal clothes again. In some cultures, the men mark their new status as hajjis by dyeing their beards bright orange with henna.

The farewell

Pilgrims may take the chance to visit other religious sites, and may also go to Madinah, where the Prophet lies buried in what used to be Aishah's room (the *hujurah*), along with Abu Bakr and Umar.

Near by is the cemetery of al-Baqi where many of his family and the early Companions are buried (including his daughter Fatimah, grandson Hasan and the Caliph Uthman). The tombs are now simply mounds of small stones – the historic mausoleums were destroyed by the strict Islamic Wahhabi sect in the reign of King Abd al-Aziz al-Saud.

Highlights of the Muslim year

For Sunni Muslims, there are only two major religious festivals in the Islamic calendar – Eid ul-Fitr, the feast that breaks the fast at the end of Ramadan, and Eid ul-Adha, which takes place during the Hajj. They are times of celebration and joy, when family and friends get together and the local community feels a strong sense of fellowship with the whole Muslim world. Shi'ite Muslims also celebrate the Day of Ashura in the month of Muharram (see pp. 87–8).

The word 'eid' (or 'id') comes from an Arab word meaning 'returning at regular intervals'. Eids do not take place on the same date each year, however, because the Muslim year is lunar, and shorter than the solar year by 11 days. Therefore, the Islamic festival days are not seasonal and cannot have fixed dates.

The regular return of Eid is an important feature, for it gives the opportunity every year to remember family, friends and loved ones, to mend damaged relationships, and forgive enemies, do things that have been put off or forgotten, and send greetings and renew contacts with people not seen for a long time. A conscious effort is made to see that no one is left lonely or depressed, and the rich are expected to give the poor the means to have their feast too, with a special donation known as zakat ul-fitr.

Eid ul-Fitr

The Ramadan fast ends the night before the Eid day. Its date depends on the sighting of the new moon, which has caused some confusion in countries where the night sky is not always clear. This is always a source of irritation to those involved in planning such things as school diaries in advance. Many Muslims feel that scientific calculations should be used to make the whole matter beyond dispute.

The end of the fast is signalled by the call to prayer from the mosque, by the firing of cannons and guns, or the beating of drums. The time is also announced on radio and TV in Islamic societies, and mosques get the news by radio, telex and telephone (if one can get through, since many switchboards become jammed at this time). After the signal or sighting, there is a great release of emotion and much hugging, handshaking and kissing. The fast is traditionally broken with something very simple, usually dates or other fruit, and fruit drinks or milk; then the *maghrib* prayer is said.

In Muslim countries there is no work or school on *Eid* days. Everyone going to *Eid* prayer first takes a full bath or shower, and then dresses in new or best clothes. These prayers command huge gatherings in the largest mosque in the area, or the principal mosque of the city, known as the *jami'a* mosque. Sometimes surrounding roads are cleared of traffic so that people overflowing from the mosque can pray in the street. In many places there are open fields called *Eid gahs*, or maybe a park, playing-field or car park – any large open space where a very big crowd can gather. Women and children are encouraged to attend.

The *salat ul-fitr* prayer consists of two *rakat* with extra *takbirs* (saying of 'Allahu Akbar') and a sermon, usually about giving charity. There is no call to prayer. The first of these prayers comes an hour after sunrise, and others may be arranged up to midday. After the prayer, everyone greets each other with '*Eid Mubarak*' (meaning '*to you be the blessings of Eid*'), hugs and kisses, and then the visiting of friends and family begins. Children receive presents and pocket money.

At midday there is a large meal, the first during the day for over a month! It may have to be in several sittings if relays of guests arrive. Luckily, the Middle Eastern style of cookery lends itself to these large feasts, and it is fairly easy to expand the food to fit the numbers that turn up.

During the afternoon, families often visit the cemetery to remember their beloved dead, and sit by their graves for a while.

The day ends with more visiting and entertaining, going on late into the night.

Eid ul-Adha

This is the 'Major festival', the 'Feast of Sacrifice'. It can last four days, and is celebrated at the end of the Hajj in commemoration of Ibrahim's obedience and triumph over the temptations of the devil. It is a serious occasion, symbolizing the submission of each individual Muslim, and the renewal of total commitment to Allah.

The slaughter of an animal is not intended in any way as a propitiatory sacrifice to God, but as meat for a communal feast. In the West, trained licence-holders must go to a proper slaughterhouse to sacrifice on behalf of the community. Although newspapers sometimes print horrifying stories of Muslims slaughtering sheep or goats in their backyards, the perpetrators are usually newcomers who are unaware of the law or the facilities provided.

Muharram and Ashura

The first month of the Muslim year is Muharram. It commemorates the departure of the Prophet to Madinah, the event that marked the turning-point for Islam, following Caliph Umar's decision to date the start of the year back to Muharram. Muslims also date their years from this year, and call them AH – after the *Hijrah*. On New Year's Day (1st Muharram) Muslims think of 'migrating' from their past to their future, putting old sins and failings behind them and making a fresh start with New Year resolutions.

The 10th Muharram, known as 'Ashura', celebrates various aspects of deliverance – the day when Nuh (Noah) left the Ark after the Flood to begin new life on earth, the birth of Ibrahim and the day on which he was supposed to sacrifice Isma'il, the day on which Ayyub (Job) was released from his suffering, the day on which God saved Moses from Pharaoh, the day on which

Jesus was born, and the day on which the Day of Judgement is expected. Fasting is not obligatory, but most do keep a day's fast.

Ashura is a particularly significant day for Shi'ite Muslims, for it was on this day, in 680, that the Prophet's heroic grandson Husayn (along with 72 other members of the Prophet's family) was martyred at Karbala by the troops of the Sunni Umayyad Caliph Yazid. Shi'ites parade in dramatic processions led by a white horse, with floats depicting the events, and perform plays. Some of the more fervent beat themselves with chains and cut their flesh, to share in his sufferings in a small way, a practice officially discouraged. Sunni Muslims do not revere Husayn with the same fervour – to them, he was but one among many noble martyrs.

Milad an-Nabi

The Prophet's birthday is traditionally celebrated on 12th Rabi'ul-Awwal (in Western dating it was probably on 20th August, 570). There is some controversy among Muslims as to whether this day should be celebrated because it is an innovation, introduced by the Abbasid caliphs of Baghdad and made popular by the Sufis in the 10th century. Purists feel it is over-veneration to celebrate a human being, no matter how much loved and respected. Others feel it is wrong not to commemorate the birth of such a great prophet.

Laylat ul-Miraj

This night (27th Rajab) commemorates the Prophet's night journey to Jerusalem and ascent through the heavens to the throne of God (whether

> **must know**
>
> It is preferable if all the members of all the mosques in a locality can join together for *Eid* prayers.

Procession of Shi'ites self-flagellating with chains for Ashura, Iran.

miraculous or visionary, see p. 19). Many Muslims will spend the entire night reading the Qur'an and praying. In some countries the mosques are illuminated for this night. Others reject all this as innovation.

Laylat ul-Bara'at

This is the 'Night of Blessing', or the 'Night of the Decree', celebrated on the night of the full moon before the start of Ramadan. It is Muslim tradition that on this night God makes His orders known to the angels as to who will live and who will die, whose sins will be forgiven and who will be condemned. The Prophet used to begin his preparations for Ramadan by staying awake in prayer throughout this night, as do many Muslims also to this day. The following day it is traditional to visit the graves of departed loved ones, to pray for their souls. Sometimes a special meal is eaten, and candles are lit. Sweets are made, and sweets and loaves distributed among the poor. Many Muslims fast for two days. Others reject all these practices as innovation.

Laylat ul-Qadr

This is the Night of Power, on which the Prophet received his first message from God through the angel Jibril, in the cave on Mount Nur. It is usually celebrated on the 27th Ramadan with a night of prayer at the mosque.

want to know more?

Read the following articles in *Saudi Arabia Spring 2000 Magazine* at www.saudiembassy.net/Publications/MagSpring00/HAJJ.htm
• 'The HAJJ: A Pilgrimage to Makkah'
• 'Saudi Arabia: Impact of the Hajj', by David Long
• And a pragmatic look at some difficult conditions: 'The Faith & the Filth: Performing Hajj in 1427'
• To hear the call to prayer from the Umayyad Mosque in Damascus, go to: www.youtube.com/watch?v=IMDKpwdmelc

5 Where Muslims worship

The Muslim place of prayer is known as a mosque, or *masjid* (literally, a 'place of bowing down'). It does not have to be a special building – the Prophet said simply that, 'The whole world has been made a place of prayer, pure and clean.' In this chapter you will learn about places where Muslims pray, the functions of a community mosque, special features, both outside and in, and how to behave in a mosque, as well as glimpsing some very famous mosques.

Where Muslims worship

The Prophet said: 'Wherever the hour of prayer overtakes you, perform it. That place is a mosque.'

must know

Britain's oldest mosque was founded in 1889 by the converted lawyer Abdullah Quilliam in Liverpool; the oldest surviving mosque, paid for by Queen Victoria's friend the Begum of Bhopal, is in Woking, Surrey. It was also established in 1889.

Buildings for worship

In Muslim countries it is quite normal to see people praying by the roadside, or at places such as railway stations, or in little areas set aside for prayer marked out by a few stones, perhaps with a mat to kneel on. You might also see something that looks like a weather-vane, indicating the direction of Makkah to the stranger. If possible, there will be a water supply near at hand for ritual washing, although *tayammum* is acceptable for the traveller.

The first mosques were extremely rudimentary, perhaps comprising no more than a level place cleared of sharp stones, large enough for the Muslim community to kneel together and place their heads on the earth; a water supply, if possible; and a means of summoning the faithful to prayer – usually by calling from a nearby rooftop, or from the highest part of the mosque (either a flat roof or a tower constructed for this purpose). A shady study or rest area was also appreciated, and some sort of lighting for prayers that took place during the hours of darkness (the *fajr* and *isha)*. The first mosques were simply lit by burning straw.

The main types of mosque

As Muslim architecture developed, three types predominated – the hypostyle, central or multiple dome, and *iwan*.

Page 90: Iwan of Masjid-e-Eman, Isfahan, Iran.

Almost every large mosque contains a courtyard known as a *sahn*, which is surrounded on all sides by rooms and sometimes an arcade. *Sahns* usually feature a central pool known as a *howz*, used for performing ablutions.

Hypostyle or Arab-type mosques were square or rectangular, with enclosed courtyards and covered prayer halls for shelter. The roofs were supported by columns and arches. Hypostyle mosques frequently also have outer arcades, for extra shade. Most mosques of this type were constructed during the Umayyad and Abbasid dynasties (see pp. 134-7).

The Mezquita (Spanish, from the Arabic *masjid*) was a famous hypostyle mosque in Córdoba, now a Roman Catholic cathedral. Its most distinctive feature is the forest of over 850 columns supporting its huge ceiling. The Moors took them ready-made from other sources, but as these columns were only 3 metres high, they invented the double-tiered column-and-arch construction, so increasing the height of the ceiling.

In a central-dome mosque, the space over the prayer-hall is dominated by one huge central dome, possibly surrounded by smaller and lower semi-domes. This design was introduced by the Ottomans in the 15th century, and was heavily influenced by Byzantine religious architecture.

The *iwan* mosque was the typical Persian design, based on pre-Islamic Iranian architecture. Many started life as converted Zoroastrian fire temples, where the courtyard (which serves as

did you know?

Al-Mansur (*c.* 938-1002), a ruler of Muslim Spain, led a raid as far north as Santiago de Compostela and carried off the church's bells to Córdoba, to have them melted down and made into lamps for the mosque. When Ferdinand III reconquered Córdoba, his first act was to take the lamps back to St James's shrine, where they were turned back into bells.

The *sahn* of the Great Mosque, Damascus, Syria.

The minaret and
domes of the
Mevlana Rumi's
mosque, Qonya,
Turkey.

the prayer-hall) was used to house the sacred fire.
This was the most popular type of mosque in the
medieval period, and remained dominant in Persia
(Iran). The courtyard is surrounded by two-storeyed
verandahs behind which are situated small rooms for
teachers and students. From the middle of each side
run vaulted halls, the *iwans*, usually twice as high as
the adjacent parts of the building, open to the front and
roofed. A smaller *iwan* of the same type serves as the
gateway. The main *iwan* often contains the founder's
tomb and is crowned with a dome (frequently
gilded). The walls of these mosques are always
overlaid with mosaics and smooth tiles decorated
with carved Arabic script and flower arabesques.

External and internal features

Mosques do not necessarily look like mosques.
None of the traditional architectural features is
compulsory. Where the mosque is purpose-built,

it is most recognizable by its dome and the minaret. The dome is usually directly over the prayer hall, a feature that reminds Muslims of their Middle-Eastern origins. It is an architectural device giving an impression of space and calm inside.

The use of domes spans centuries, first appearing in 591 with the golden Dome of the Rock (Qubbat al-Sakhrah) in Jerusalem. Most early domes were small, but gradually became bigger until they encompassed the entire roof above the prayer-hall. The Mughals popularized onion-shaped domes, which are seen in South Asia and Persia (see the picture on p. 143).

Domes are often decorated both inside and out with beautiful tiles in geometric designs. Inside, they draw one's attention upwards, towards the heavens, and God. They also ensure wonderful acoustics.

A minaret is a tall, slender tower attached to or built near the mosque. It has a balcony from which the *mu'adhin* calls the faithful to prayer. The word minaret comes from *nur*, meaning 'light'.

In pre-Islamic Arabia, minarets served as beacons or markers to guide caravan routes, and as light-houses along coastlines. Standing vertically, it serves as a spiritual symbol that links heaven and earth.

Atop the dome or the minaret one can often see the symbol of Islam, a crescent moon. Sometimes there is also a five-pointed star, which reminds Muslims of the 'Five Pillars' of their faith. The moon reminds them of God the Creator, and the lunar calendar, which governs Islamic festivals.

Inside the mosque

Most noticeable straight away is the lack of furniture. Everyone kneels or sits on the floor. Pictorial

did you know?

The first Islamic minaret was constructed in Basra in 665 during the reign of the Umayyad Caliph Mu'awiyyah. The tallest minaret in the world is located at the King Hassan II Mosque in Casablanca, Morocco.

decorations and statues are forbidden, because it is thought to encourage idolatry. However, mosques are not necessarily dull. Many are extremely beautiful – with richly coloured carpets, different marbles for columns and surfaces, intricately patterned and colourful tiles, carved woodwork, stained glass, chandeliers, gold-painted ceilings and decorated domes, ornamental calligraphy, and so forth.

The concept of Allah's infinite power is evoked by designs with repeating themes, pattern and geometry, which suggest infinity.

The carpet in the prayer-hall is generally marked with regular patterns, so that when the prayer lines

Mosque in Oslo, Norway, with prayer-time clocks, *mihrab*, *minbar*, and a carpet patterned to look like individual prayer-mats.

form, people know where to stand and how much space to occupy. Some massive carpets have patterns resembling individual prayer-mats. However, when a large congregation comes together for prayer, the people form up very close together, shoulder-to-shoulder, and often literally toe-to-toe, with their toes touching those of the next person.

A series of clocks usually shows the prayer times each day. Times are flexible for personal prayer, but a strict timetable is necessary when congregations come together. The clocks will show the five *salat* and the Friday prayer.

Washing facilities

It is not necessary to perform *wudu* at the mosque, and many Muslims prefer to do it at home. In the mosque, men and women usually have separate facilities. The most common arrangement is a row of taps set in the wall over a drain, with stools arranged for people to sit on while they wash their feet. People coming to pray often leave the water to dry on them, without using towels.

The focal point in any mosque is the niche faced during prayer that indicates the direction of Makkah, the *qiblah*. This is often an alcove in the wall, known as a *mihrab*, and may be beautifully decorated. The imam stands in front of the *mihrab*.

When buildings have been converted into mosques, the *qiblah* may seem to be in a very odd place, not at all a focal point – but it always indicates the direction of Makkah. Some large mosques have a *dikka*, a platform, usually made of carved wood in line with the *mihrab*, for the *mu'adhins*, who chant in unison with the imam as he prays.

On the right side of the *mihrab* is the *minbar*, the elevated platform or pulpit from which the imam addresses the congregation in his sermons. These can be very simple, or highly ornate. The simplest are usually just a couple of carpeted steps with a small platform at the top. Ornate *minbars* can consist of a high flight of stairs, beautifully carved and decorated, made of wood, stone, marble and alabaster.

What are mosques used for?

First and foremost, the mosque is the place where Muslims gather to pray together. But it is also a very important part of the social life of the Muslim community too. Modern mosques run homework clubs, women's activities and youth clubs, and may have IT facilities, computers, crêches and kitchens. Once the prayers are over, Muslims often stay on, chatting to their friends or, if the mosque has a 'social' room, youngsters play snooker or table tennis. The imam can use the premises to meet people, discuss problems, or help with family life.

Most mosques have a collection of books – sometimes enough to qualify as a library. Visiting speakers are often invited for talks, or to discuss problems of Muslim law.

The mosque also fulfils an important function as the school or *madrassah* where people can study the Arabic language, the Qur'an and various Islamic subjects. All Muslims are expected to learn as much of the Qur'an as they are able, and for many this is a difficult business, as Arabic is not their first language. Children usually start these Islamic studies at the age of five, and continue until they are 15 or so. It is quite possible to go on studying for the rest of your life. Arabic classes and Qur'an study classes (known as *tafsir*) are held every day, and children usually go straight after school, studying for around two hours, five nights per week. Some schools even demand weekend work, too.

Mosques can also be used for all sorts of functions – meetings, weddings and festival days, birthdays, or parties celebrating circumcision, home-coming, or the passing of an important exam. These are all joyful functions. Most mosques will have a good kitchen area as part of the complex, and perhaps a special function room. Some even run a café for the public.

Sometimes people sleep overnight in a mosque, either on the carpeted floor of the prayer-hall or in specially provided facilities. Mosques may offer services to the community as primitive hospitals, feeding centres or 'rest-rooms'. The mosque may also have an ablutions room where it is possible to administer the last washing to the deceased before shrouding takes place.

Visiting a mosque

Visitors should be suitably dressed – clean, smart and tidy. It is polite for women to cover their arms and legs, and many show respect by covering their hair. Both men and women must remove their shoes, and may have to sit on the floor. There will probably be two entrances, one for men and one for women. In many mosques men and women pray in separate areas, and how this is arranged depends on the design. Sometimes the women have a balcony, or pray behind a curtain at the back. Quiet, respectful behaviour is expected at all times. Muslims pray two *rakat* before the *salah* prayer to 'greet the mosque'.

want to know more?

• Ismail Serageldin and James Steele (eds), *Architecture of the contemporary mosque*, 1996
• On the net: Islamic Architecture from the Middle East – www.vam.ac.uk/ collections/asia/islamic _gall/index.html
• For Damascus tours and calling the adhan, see www.panoramas .dk/fullscreen6/f47-damascus.html

6 Islamic law

Islamic law is known as the Shari'ah (the 'way' or 'the path to the water source'), the legal framework within which Muslim public and private life and law, worship, and standards of morals are regulated. It guides Muslims as they strive to carry out God's will in every aspect of life (including politics, economics, banking, business, contracts, sexuality, hygiene and social issues), and helps them to judge what is right and wrong according to Islam. In this chapter you will read about the sources of this law, the way it is applied, the schools of thought, and some details of Islamic jurisprudence.

Islamic law

Islamic law is unique in that it claims to be of divine rather than human origin. Secular law consists of texts that are interpreted by lawyers and judges, subject to the influences of time and place, the pressures of interest-groups, public mood, and other factors. Such laws change over time. This is not the case in Islamic law.

must know

The *hadiths* are a huge body of traditions, at first handed down by oral transmission, but their authenticity became endangered by pious fabrications and inaccuracies. Following investigation by specialist scholars, they were arranged into categories – such as 'sound', 'good' or 'weak'. The scholars known as Bukhari (d. 870) and Muslim (d. 875) produced critical collections that have ever since been regarded as most trustworthy. The works of Abu Dawud (d. 999), Nasa'i (d. 915), Tirmidhi (d.892) and Ibn Majah (d.896) completed the 'authentic collections', known together as the 'Six Books'.

The basis of Islamic law

Islamic jurisprudence is based on three major sources. The first is the *nass*, the explicit textual rulings of Islam. They derive from two sources – the *ahkam* (plural of *hukm*, meaning 'command'), about 500 verses of the Qur'an that are specific commands and beyond dispute; and the *sunnah* – the Prophet's practices, rulings and teachings derived from the *hadiths*. If there was no clear ruling on a particular matter in the Qur'an, Muslims were commanded to obey the Prophet, and refer disputes either to him or those he set over them (Surah 4.59). From the *ahkam* and *sunnat* are derived all the principles behind the law, and any inferred or implied meanings.

Some of the *ahkam* are particular and some are general, but they do not cover every eventuality – many modern-day issues simply did not exist when the collections were made. Therefore, scholars have to infer the general principles and intentions *behind* the particular commands to apply them appropriately.

The second source of Islamic jurisprudence is therefore *ijtihad* (the exercise of conscience and reason), and *ijma* (the consensus among the jurists on specific legal questions if they are not addressed in the Qur'an or *sunnah*, or are answered in seemingly contradictory terms). For conservative Muslims, the only *ijma* regarded as binding (like a Qur'anic command) are those made by the first caliphs, who had been the Prophet's closest Companions.

In Sunni Islam, the third source of jurisprudence is *qiyas* – the process of analogical reasoning aimed at extending a given ruling from a known to a new injunction, provided that the precedent and the new problem both share the same effective cause (the *hikmah*) – the specific set of circumstances that triggered a certain law into action. For example, the injunction against drinking alcohol could be extended to taking cocaine – since alcohol was forbidden because it intoxicates, harms, and removes Muslims from mindfulness of God, and cocaine does the same.

Rules and concepts conceived on the basis of *qiyas* or other reasoning skills are always subject to change, since human judgement is not infallible.

A recurring theme in Shi'a jurisprudence is the vital use of logic (*mantiq*) and intellect (*aql*) in determining whether a derived conclusion is compatible with Qur'an and *sunnah*.

The five categories

In Islam, a particular issue or course of action cannot always be ruled simply right or wrong. There are not just two categories of behaviour to choose from, but five:

• *fard* or *wajib* – things that are compulsory and *must* be done, such as keeping the Five Pillars (see p. 65), telling the truth;

• *haram* – things that are forbidden and should never be done, such as committing adultery, eating pork, being dishonest;

Page 100: Door knocker on a mosque in Seville, Spain.

must know

Fiqh, from the word for 'intelligence' or 'knowledge', means the whole process of Islamic law as developed by Muslim jurists.

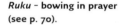

Ruku – bowing in prayer (see p. 70).

• *mandub or mustahab* – actions that are recommended but not compulsory, such as giving charity, visiting the sick, fostering an orphan;

• *makruh* – actions that are not actually forbidden, but are disliked or disapproved of, such as divorce, smoking cigarettes, social snobbery;

• *mubah* – actions decided by conscience because there is no clear guidance, such as following secular law, watching TV, playing pop music, using birth control.

Anything that is either compulsory or forbidden to a Muslim is always specifically stated in the Qur'an, and there is no ambiguity. If something has not been specifically forbidden, it is permitted, under the guidance of Islamic principles and conscience. Most problems pertaining to modern life fall in the *mubah* section. However, it is possible for many actions to fall into more than one category depending on the circumstances, and that is where knowledge of Islamic principles (*usul al-fiqh* – the roots of the law) come into play.

Take an issue such as contraception. It is forbidden in the Qur'an to kill children, but this ruling was given to stop the nomadic Bedouin practice of leaving infants (usually girls) they could not maintain out in the desert to die or burying them alive. This injunction could be extended to unborn children, and thus prohibit abortion. Birth control that aborts is therefore forbidden, but that which prevents conception is not ruled upon.

If contraception is a deliberate attempt to thwart the will of God, it is *haram*. If the woman would die if she became pregnant, it would be permitted. If she already had numerous children and was too poor to feed them, it might be recommended. If she was merely worried that getting pregnant would spoil her figure, it would be disapproved of.

Madhhabs

A school of jurisprudence is known as a *madhhab*. By the third century after the life of the Prophet four major schools had developed in Sunni Islam, and they still remain to this day – the Hanifi, Maliki, Hanbali and Shafi'i, named after the most eminent jurists of that early period.

The main Shi'ite schools are the earlier Ja'fari (named after Abu Hanifah's teacher), and the Zaydi, Ibadi and Thahiri. Thus, on any point of law, there could be at least 10 different opinions, and a considerable amount of debate.

Generally, Sunni Muslims prefer one *madhhab* to the others (normally a regional preference), and some feel that only their particular *madhhab* has the truth. Some even insist on *taqlid*, the unquestioning acceptance of rulings from their higher religious authorities without requiring technical proofs or seeking further development. This practice is very common amongst Sufi mystics.

Others maintain it is perfectly acceptable to pick and choose from a range of schools (which was indeed the original practice), or even found a new one. To adhere just to one is to narrow one's source of experience and knowledge. Experts study the evidences and opinions of many schools.

Conservative Muslims are uneasy about the present-day urge to abandon the scholars and 'return' to the 'simple faith' of Qur'an and *sunnah*, seeing this as the abandonment of centuries of detailed, case-by-case Islamic scholarship by highly

did you know?

A *fatwa* is a legal opinion or verdict given by a qualified jurist. In Western media the word is often misused to mean a death sentence (for example, the *fatwa* against the writer Salman Rushdie), but it really means any clarification on any new or unprecedented case for which there is no clear directive either in Qur'an or *sunnah*. The word is the Arabic plural of *fata*, or 'new boy' – it is used to refer to anything young, new, unfamiliar and unprecedented.

sophisticated specialists, Qur'anic exegetes, lexicographers and other masters of the Islamic legal sciences, to follow contemporary sheikhs who might have less knowledge and insight.

Some extreme *madhhab* followers believe all possible decisions have already been ruled upon, and the 'gate of *ijtihad*' should be closed, whereas other Muslims wish to see scope for fresh thought, and the 'gate' remaining open to allow the brains of modern scholars to inject new impetus. Shi'ites certainly accept that living scholars have just as much right to interpret Divine Law as those of the past.

The right to interpret

Who is qualified to interpret Islam for today? Many conservative Muslims wish to keep the *ulama* (plural of *alim*, 'teacher') as a self-perpetuating class, confining the right to interpret and explain Islam to qualified jurists. They are opposed to the use of reasoning by unqualified persons. Human rulers or interpreters may claim that they have the right or ability to change law, but to a conservative this smacks of an arrogant challenge to the sovereignty of Allah, and the authority of the Shari'ah. They maintain that human reason should only be used as a last resort in the understanding of the Will of God, employed only when the texts are silent and if no medieval scholar has previously addressed the issue.

But Islamic modernists believe that 'closing the gate of *ijtihad*' has resulted in intellectual stultification, and do not wish to be slavishly bound to the interpretations of earlier Muslim *madhhabs*. The quest for truth now requires a multi-disciplinary

approach and expertise through many sources –
science, rationalism, human experience, critical
thinking and so on. They feel that there should be a
restoration of reason, personal responsibility, the
opportunity for the individual interpretation of texts,
and the encouragement of democracy, which would
bring back the concept of *shura* (consultation) and
defeat corrupt and oppressive tyranny.

The way forward
Ijtihad includes subsidiary legal principles such as
equity (*istihsan*) and general welfare or public
interest (*islah, maslahah*). One major reason why
fundamentalist extremism is so dangerous is that it
tends to curtail the development of Shari'ah by
seeking to preserve the strict adherence to one
school of thought, and the letter of the law as
opposed to the spirit, and thus becomes archaic and
inadequate for dealing with developing issues. In
some societies, this has resulted in situations where
the imposition of Shari'ah law has become cruel and
unjust. This nearly always stems from extremely
conservative jurists blindly imitating medieval
practices without considering the contexts within
which they were constructed.

Reformers therefore see the need to look very closely
at the timeless *principles* of the laws – not just the
text, but the *context* of the text, the broader principles
and values underlying the rulings of the Qur'an.

The *Hadd* Laws (the *Hudud*)
The *hadd* laws (pl. *hudud*) are the 'laws of limit' or
'restriction', whose purpose is to curtail aspects of

must know

The word *madhhab* is
derived from 'to go' or
'to take as a way', and a
person or student on
that way is a *mujtahid*. A
madhhab represents the
entire school of thought
of a particular *mujtahid*
imam, together with the
scholars that came after
them who were able to
check their reasoning
and refine and upgrade
their work.

human behaviour. They are God-given rulings. In man-made law, something seen as a heinous act (and therefore a crime) at one time may become socially acceptable and not a crime at all, and not punished in another (e.g. homosexuality and abortion in the UK). This is not so for the *hudud*.

Hadd Law covers six specific matters:

- *zinah* (adultery and fornication)
- *qadhf* (slander, false accusation)
- *sariqah* (larceny or theft, or taking by stealth)
- *hirabah* (taking with force, kidnapping, armed robbery, terrorism, waging war against the state)
- *sukr* (consumption of alcohol)
- *riddah* (apostasy – see box, opposite)

Behaviour that falls short of God's requirements but happens in private is generally left as a matter between that individual and God – Muslims are not encouraged to go round spying on people.

So, if a Muslim got drunk or indulged in sexual immorality (which includes homosexuality, incidentally) with another consenting adult, it would most certainly indicate not only lack of belief in the real existence of God, but also that the believer had extremely weak discipline, or cared little or nothing for the consequences come the Day of Judgement; but this state of affairs could potentially change at any time.

Unless there were reliable witnesses (and *four* witnesses are needed for sexual immorality), the judgement of that individual would be left to God, in the hope that the Muslim might genuinely repent, in which case, God would always forgive (even if offended humans felt unable to). But if a Muslim broke the law in public, or their private behaviour involved abusing or harming or causing offence to another, it becomes subject to legal penalty. Muslims found guilty and convicted in a court of law face punishment according to three possible categories, depending on the type of offence committed and the strength of the evidence: *hadd* – specific penalty; *jinayah* – retaliation or compensation; and *ta'zir* – discretionary penalty.

The *hadd* penalties for some crimes could be very severe, and are the reason for today's concern about barbarity in Islamic law. In fact, it was hoped that punishment for these things should be unnecessary in a truly Muslim society, since Muslims would find such conduct beneath them. Non-Muslims were not expected to keep the very high standards, and therefore should not be subject to the *hadd*.

If a Muslim deliberately committed theft, the punishment could include the amputation of a hand (followed by amputation of other limbs if thieving continued). Illicit sexual intimacy earned a beating, and the death penalty could be given for murder, treason, adulterous intercourse performed in public, and apostasy where it involved treason or warfare (*hirabah* – 5.32-33). It was not given for simply abandoning Islam as many (including Muslims) have wrongly assumed.

The Law of Moses had allowed the death sentence of stoning for adultery, and a few Muslims were executed by this means in the lifetime of the Prophet. Interestingly, they were convicted because they had insisted themselves, four times, that they were guilty, and preferred the punishment in this life to facing Allah in the state of sin in the life to come. There is no verse requiring stoning in the Qur'an.

A moment of private prayer.

The *hadiths* give us this example of the Prophet's *sunnah*. A child labourer who was paid a pittance by his employer stole fruit from his garden to eat. He was caught and hauled in front of the Prophet by the irate employer, demanding that his hand should be cut off. The Prophet decided that the child was underpaid and undernourished, and instead of punishing him, made the employer promise to educate the child and provide proper food for him until he grew up.

A famous case history reported in two *hadith* collections told of Ma'idh ibn Malik, a man who insisted on confessing despite the Prophet's attempts to turn away from him, and investigation into whether he was of sound mind. When his punishment commenced, Ma'idh tried to break free but was killed by a pursuer hurling a camel bone at him. The Prophet was not pleased. 'Why did you not leave him alone?' he said. 'Perhaps he might have repented, and then he would have been forgiven by Allah.'

Jinayah penalties cover homicide and bodily harm, which are punishable either by *qisas* (retaliation to satisfy justice to the victim, based on the principle of 'an eye for an eye', which could also, therefore, include the death penalty) or payment of *diyah* (blood-money or money compensation). *Ta'zir* (corrective) penalties are the least serious (although not always) and can be applied where there is no specific *hadd* or *qisas* penalty, or when the proof is based on a strong assumption of guilt but is not enough to impose specific penalties.

In fact, Islamic law requires a very high level of proof for the most serious crimes, which gives ample scope for defence procedure. Judges are expected to study all mitigating circumstances to the best of their ability – and if there is doubt (*shubhah*), the *hadd* sentence must be commuted to that of *ta'zir*, for which there are lesser punishments such as reprimand, threat (being bound over), boycott, public disclosure, fines, working in repayment, seizure of property, confinement in the home or place of detention, and flogging. Consuming alcohol and committing apostasy are usually treated as *ta'zir* crimes because no clear specific penalty was given in the Qur'an.

The Prophet taught mercy if it were possible, but could not be bribed or wheedled out of giving fair judgement. He once stated bluntly that even if his own beloved daughter Fatimah committed theft, he would not hesitate but would cut her hand off himself.

In Shari'ah law, properly applied, all people are equal, no matter how humble or rich and influential. People are not culpable if they are not conscious of what they have done, or the balance of their mind is disturbed, or they have not yet reached puberty (Surah 4.135). Islamic justice should not be administered blindly but tempered with mercy, following all the principles of fairness (4.135 and 5.8), and defendants are innocent until proven guilty (24.15 and 39.7), giving them the right to be heard and to appeal (24.24, 82.11, 36.69-70), and have legal representation.

Justice can only prevail when legal scholars take a broad approach to the law and adhere to its spirit, rather than to its letter, so that it does not seem outrageous. That is the approach consistent with the concept of *istislah*, the practice of using legal reasoning to interpret the law in the light of Islam's general principles of serving the public good (*maslahah mursalah*).

Modern reformers emphasize that by questioning the relevance of the modes of punishment prescribed in *hudud* they are not challenging the notion of right and wrong that underpins Islamic law, and have never raised doubts about the validity of Qur'anic values and principles. After all, *hudud* laws may set a code of conduct, but they can never bring about a change of character.

want to know more?

• Laleh Bakhtiar and Kevin Reinhart, *Encyclopedia of Islamic Law: A Compendium of the Major Schools*, Kazi Publications, 1996
• Khaled Abou El Fadl, *Reasoning with God: Rationality and Thought in Islam*, Oneworld Publications, 2003
• Omid Safi, *Progressive Muslims: On Justice, Gender, and Pluralism*, Oneworld Publications, 2003
• Abdul Hakam Murad, *Understanding the Four Madhhabs*, Cambridge, 1999
• J. Esposito and N. Delong-Bas, *Women in Muslim Family Law*, 2002

7 The Islamic world view

To Muslims, every aspect of life on earth, their place within the home, their community, their country and the world is governed by awareness of God. In this chapter we will look at the Muslim family and the individual rites of passage – from conception, birth and circumcision, to adolescence, sexuality and adulthood, with its issues of marriage and roles and rights of husband and wife, to the end of life, death and burial. We will also examine the concepts of *halal* and *haram*, things which are allowed or forbidden, as they relate to food and drink, clothing, employment, wealth and poverty, slavery, and care of the environment.

The Islamic world view

In Islam, the family was ordained by God as the right way for us to live with and care for each other. Maintaining a family needs constant work, compassion, a sense of duty and order, and a willingness to sacrifice freedom and selfish enjoyment. It is thus the basis of the moral and social values of society at large.

must know

The Prophet said: 'The most valuable of treasures is a good wife. She is pleasing to her husband's eyes, obedient to his word, and watchful over his possessions in his absence. And the best of you are those who treat your wives best.'

The importance of family

For a Muslim, 'family' includes grandparents, aunts and uncles, and cousins. The man is responsible for trying to support a household that is intended as the safe haven for those in his care, and a woman is expected to be responsible for running it with love, efficiency and cleanliness, even if she also goes out to work.

The most important person in a Muslim family is the mother. A home that is the sanctum of a good mother is a blessed home. The Prophet taught that Paradise lay at the feet of mothers, and they should always be treasured. The mother sets the standard for morality, politeness and her children's first lessons in Islam.

Birth

A newly created person is not an 'accident' or a 'mistake' but a gift from God.

Abortion is forbidden (unless continuing the pregnancy would put the mother's life in danger), and so is any form of contraception that is a form of abortion rather than prevention of conception. Should conception take place, Muslims must accept that it is God's will for the child to be born.

Page 112: Detail, the Alhambra, Granada, Spain.

As soon as a baby is born it is welcomed into the family of Islam, the *ummah*. The call to prayer (the *adhan*) is whispered into the baby's right ear, and the command to rise and worship (the *iqamah*) into the left.

Next, the baby's mouth is rubbed with a little honey, sweet juice or chewed date, in a ceremony known as *tahnik*. This is to symbolize the wish that the child will be 'sweet' (obedient and kind).

At the end of its first week comes the *aqiqah*. The baby's head is shaved and the weight of the hair in silver or gold is given to the poor. Even if the baby is bald as an egg, Muslim parents usually still donate to charity. Sweets are sent to friends and neighbours to celebrate. It is also traditional to hold a feast and share meat – two animals are the customary offering for a boy and one for a girl. (None of the above is compulsory practice.)

The baby should then be given a Muslim name. The Prophet commented that the name most pleasing to God was Abdullah ('servant of God'); the baby could also be declared a 'servant of God' by being given one of His special Names, such as Abdul Rahman (servant of the 'Compassionate One').

The baby's parents also get a new name – they are entitled to drop their own names and take a *kunya*, which means they are called 'father of' or 'mother of' whatever their eldest child's name is. So, if Muhammad and Zaynab have a son they call Umar, they become Abu Umar and Umm Umar.

The next thing, for a healthy boy baby, is circumcision, or *khitan*, the cutting of the foreskin at the end of the penis. Jews and Muslims regard this as one of God's key commands, a practice commenced

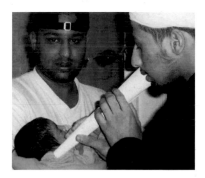

Whispering the *adhan* into a newborn baby's ear.

A Turkish boy dressed up for his circumcision party.

must know

Female circumcision –
actually female genital
mutilation – has nothing
to do with Islam but is a
barbarous cultural
practice that predates
Islam.

with the prophet Ibrahim. In Turkey, it is traditional
to leave the boy until he is about 10 years old, then
dress him up like a glittering little prince and
circumcise him at a special party, so that the
circumcision becomes a rite of passage into
adolescence. This is not the practice in the rest of the
Muslim world, where the procedure is carried out
while the boy is a baby.

Some non-Muslims have recently campaigned to
have the circumcision of boy babies regarded as a
form of mutilation and banned until the boy is old
enough to have a choice in the matter.

Childhood

By the time the child is four or five they are prepared
for the Bismillah ceremony, when a senior relative or
imam tests the child to see if he/she can recite the
Surah al-Fatihah, or perhaps write the Arabic
alphabet. The child also learns how to perform *wudu*,
and begins to join in with the prayers. By the age of
10 children should be able to perform the five daily

prayers – meaningfully – on their own, should have started fasting, be familiar with Islamic manners and practices, see to personal cleanliness, and be aware that some things are *haram* (forbidden).

Sex and marriage

Sexual intimacy outside of marriage is forbidden. This is why Muslims often prefer to arrange their children's marriages while they are young and have them married as soon as they show signs of sexual desire.

Sex between married couples is a gift of God to be enjoyed as a blessing. Both partners should do their utmost to consider the happiness and fulfilment of the other – otherwise the union is not blessed, and no different from the mating of animals. Sex outside marriage (whether before, after or homosexual) can carry a severe penalty in a Muslim society. Making a good marriage is of the utmost importance – the lessons learned within marriage were said by the Prophet to be 'half the faith'.

Although Muslims hope to find a life-partner with whom they will live happily, marriage is not seen as a mystical sacrament 'made in heaven' between two perfectly attuned souls, or as a binding state that will only end at death. It is a *mithaq*, a social contract between two consenting adults of sound body and mind, in which each is answerable for their own deeds and actions.

Marriage brings rights and obligations to both partners and their families, and can only be successful when these are mutually respected and cherished. If the contract is broken, divorce becomes the right of the offended spouse.

did you know?

In some Islamic societies, a bride or her family might demand a huge marriage-settlement, so men are often not able to afford marriage until they are in their late 20s or older.

must know

Muslim boys are permitted to marry Christian and Jewish girls, but Muslim girls may not marry non-Muslims because the offspring take the religion of the father. Muslims may only marry Hindus, Buddhists, etc. if the other party agrees to convert to Islam.

Muslims are not encouraged to mix freely after they reach adolescence – this way they are less likely to feel sexual urges towards somebody before marriage. Such things cloud the mind, interrupt education, and can cause a lot of upset and misguided decisions.

First marriages are frequently arranged by caring parents wanting good, compatible partners for their children. Arranged marriage is not an Islamic requirement, but a sensible cultural practice. However, all have the right to get to know their intended, and to decline the match. Any Muslim who forces, coerces or fools someone into marrying without consent is committing *haram*.

Marriages do not have to be arranged by parents – sometimes parents are not the best people to choose good spouses for their offspring. A person who acts as a supervising guardian is known as a *wali*. Their function is to find out all the necessary information about the proposed spouses, vet them carefully and make recommendations. The couple may meet several times in chaperoned situations, and get to know each other. The Prophet advised that they should see each other until they knew *why* it was that they chose that particular person. If either side rejects the suggested partner, the rejecter can withdraw discreetly and politely.

Many Muslims marry within their own wider families, where the character and background of the intended is already well known. These days, Muslims are being alerted to the dangers of repeating first-cousin marriages over several generations, as this can increase the chances of inherited defects.

In Islamic marriage, the husband must pay an agreed sum of money or give property to his new wife so that she enters married life with something of her own (the *mahr*). A woman may put an enormous price upon herself, or she may agree to just a nominal sum, depending on the circumstances. Should the marriage fail, she keeps the *mahr* unless she has demanded an unreasonable divorce.

An Islamic wedding, or *nikah*, is a simple affair, and the bride does not have to dress up or even be there herself, if she does not wish to. All it requires is the bridegroom and his witness, and two witnesses to her uncoerced agreement, and acceptance of the offered *mahr*. A typical ceremony consists of readings from the Qur'an, and the exchange of vows or contract. No special religious official is necessary, but often the imam is present. Many wedding customs, such as the bride's dress, are matters of culture and nothing to do with Islam.

Marriages should also take place openly: '*Do not make a secret contract with them, but only in honourable terms.*' (Surah 2.235) The *walimah* (wedding party) usually takes place either at the wedding or within three days of it, to declare publicly that the bride and groom are now honourably entitled to each other.

Rights of husbands and wives

The husband is the head of the family, the wife the heart. Even if she is more intelligent, more educated, or more spiritually and morally gifted than him, she must agree to obey him (so long as what he requests

does not break Islamic principles – God is her
master, not her husband). If he ordered her to do
anything contrary to the will of God, she should
refuse to obey him.

Each partner must remain faithful, satisfying the
other's sexual urges if they are not abusive, hurtful
or unreasonable for health reasons, and not
deliberately doing things to anger them or make
them ashamed or anxious.

The wife has the right to be supported by her
husband, and is not obliged to work. Any money she
earns is hers, and if she chooses to give it to the
family, it is counted as an act of charity.

Polygamy

Multiple marriage was unrestricted and quite
normal for wealthy Jews and Arabs in pre-Islamic
Arabia. Previous prophets had practised polygamy –
David had at least 13 wives, and Solomon had 300,
with 700 concubines! It had little to do with sexual
urges, but more to do with prestige.

The changes ordained by Allah in the Qur'an were
that polygamy was forbidden for women, and men
were limited to just four wives - with certain
conditions:

• the first wife should not be hurt or disturbed under
any circumstances;

• later wives should not be a cause of distress to
earlier ones;

• equal physical intimacy (or loving passion) could
not be ruled upon, but all wives must be treated
fairly and equally as regards homes, food, clothing,
gifts, and so on. Nights had to be spent with each in
turn, unless a wife chooses to forgo her turn.

Divorce

The Qur'an makes it clear that of all the things God has allowed, divorce (*talaq*) is the most disliked (Surah 66.10). However, if the marriage contract has been broken and the relationship has failed, Islam does not force people to remain together in misery.

A Muslim has a genuine reason for divorce only if their spouse's behaviour goes against the *sunnah* of Islam – in other words, if he or she has become cruel, vindictive, abusive, unfaithful, neglectful, selfish, sexually abusive, tyrannical, perverted – and so on.

If the wife wishes for a divorce but has no grounds, it is known as *khul*, or divorce by settlement or negotiation. She may approach an imam to act on her behalf.

Custody of children in all kinds of divorce is normally granted to the mother, but the father remains responsible for their financial upkeep and must ensure that they are properly educated. He should also be involved in their choice of spouse, if possible.

must know

The Qur'an says: '*Either keep your wife honestly, or put her away from you with kindness. Do not force a woman to stay with you who wishes to leave. The man who does that only injures himself.*' (Surah 2:231)

Old age

Muslims are expected to treat the senior members of their families with respect, patience and under-standing. They are expected to look after their parents, but should not feel guilty if they need to bring in outside help.

Death and burial

Muslims should not fear death, for they know that since life is God's gift, the length of one's life is His Will. They believe that death is the start of an eternal life in a new state of being, and that God will forgive

their shortcomings. The true Muslim greets the possibility of death with the phrase *Amr Allah* – 'At Your Command, O Lord.'

To kill one's own self is just as sinful in Islam as killing any other person or creature. Muslims are expected to make full use of medical science to alleviate their sufferings, but if suffering is unavoidable, God's justice will alleviate suffering in the Life

to Come as compensation. This belief makes euthanasia (a 'good' assisted death) illogical.

At the deathbed

If possible, the bed should be turned so that it faces the direction of the Ka'bah. Prayers should not be intrusive, but as the dying person finds comfortable. When they have passed away, the eyes should be gently closed, and a prayer said, such as the Prophet's own prayer (over his cousin Abu Salamah): '*O Allah, forgive Your servant, raise him to high rank among those who are rightly guided; make him as a guardian of his descendants who survive him. Forgive us and him, O Lord of the Universe; make his grave spacious and grant him light in it.*'

must know

Rawdahs are gatherings to commemorate someone's death, held on the third day, or the 40th day, or the anniversary of the death. They are a custom rather than a compulsory requirement.

The deceased should then be given the final ritual wash as soon as possible, by the husband, wife or a family member – preferably of the same sex as the deceased. If males are washing females, or vice versa, their hands should be covered so that they do not touch the naked body. If there is no relative available, the washing is a duty that falls on any Muslim, to see it is done as decently as possible. Washing by hospital staff does not count as *wudu*.

Muslims are not obliged to give the ritual *wudu* to aborted foetuses or dead bodies that have been bomb-blasted. Martyrs are traditionally buried 'with their blood', usually shrouded in their clothes. If pilgrims die in *ihram*, they should be buried as pilgrims, with heads uncovered (for men) and faces unveiled (for women). Any debts outstanding should be paid from their estate (or settled by relatives) as soon as possible.

Shrouding

Simple cloths are used for shrouding, if possible three white winding sheets for a man, and five for a woman. These are all fastened in place round the deceased and only unfastened when he or she is laid in the grave. The face may be left visible until last farewells have been said.

The funeral prayer

The funeral prayer, or *salat ul-janaza*, has to be performed by at least one Muslim (chosen by the deceased, the imam or his deputy, or closest male relative). The prayer is made standing.

The funeral

Muslims are buried, not cremated. Everything should be respectful, with no ostentation. People should stand in respect when a procession passes, whether the deceased is Muslim or not. Processions should be conducted at a brisk walk. Muslims prefer bodies to be laid in the earth, rather than in a coffin.

In Muslim countries, graves are orientated towards Makkah. They should reach the depth of a man's chest, and preferably have a *qiblah* niche in it. A woman's body should be lowered in by men within her family, and all bodies are placed in the grave legs first. The deceased are placed on their right sides, with their faces turned in the direction of the Ka'bah, and supported so that they do not roll over on to their backs.

The fastening of the shroud is undone, and bricks, canes or leaves set in place so that no earth falls on the body. A little earth is then sprinkled into the grave, saying: '*We created you from it, and return you into it, and from it We will raise you a second time.*' (Surah 20:55) Then the earth is heaped over, while people pray.

The surface of the grave may be raised a hand's-breadth so that it will be recognized and not trodden on. It may be marked with a headstone, but elaborate tombstones and memorials are disapproved of. Prayers may be said at the graveside *for* the deceased, but not *to* them (i.e. to those considered to be 'saints'), which is a form of *shirk*, and the reason for the purist Wahhabi sect demolishing many much-loved historic graves.

Condolences and grieving

Muslims believe that the deceased are not dead, but waiting for the Day of Resurrection, when they will face judgement. Therefore, although sad when loved ones pass away, they regard too much mourning as lack of faith in Allah. Muslims are granted four months and ten days to mourn spouses, and for other deceased three days and nights. Some Muslims gather for a recitation of the entire Qur'an on behalf of the deceased, given either by one of the mourners or by someone hired to do so, although this is not a compulsory practice.

Halal and *haram*

In Islam, there are five categories of behaviour – compulsory, approved, left to the conscience of the individual, disapproved

did you know?

The Prophet ruled that if someone had been sent meat to eat, but did not know whether it was *halal*, the correct thing to do was not to refuse it, but to pray over it, and eat.

and forbidden. That which is *halal* is allowed, and that which is *haram* is forbidden. It applies to everything – personal conduct, activities, employment, clothing, food. Anything *halal* is approved by God because it is beneficial to the individual and society, and anything *haram* is forbidden by God because it is harmful, debasing, exploitative, and so on.

Food and drink

Muslims may not eat just anything. All fish, fruits, vegetables, grain and root crops are *halal*. Meat has to be slaughtered in a certain way, and Muslims are not allowed to eat meat that still contains blood, or meat from an animal that has died of natural causes, was strangled or gored or beaten to death, or been in any way offered to idols. It is forbidden for Muslims to drink alcohol.

The pig is regarded as unclean, and pig products are always *haram*. Many processed foods contain animal fats and gelatine (which is usually made from hide trimmings, including those of the pig), but some Muslims consider the avoidance of these unnecessary, for example, if a particular substance has undergone chemical change that renders it non-*haram*.

Slaughter

The Prophet taught: 'Truly, Allah has enjoined goodness in everything; so when you kill, kill in a good way and when you slaughter, slaughter in a good way. You should make sure your knives are sharp, and let the slaughtered animal die comfortably.' Muslims should keep animals kindly before their slaughter – shaded, comfortable, well fed and watered, in a place where they cannot see other animals being killed. If an animal has been kept cruelly or slaughtered cruelly, it is not *halal* to eat. The slaughter should be done with a very sharp knife across the jugular vein, so that the animal loses consciousness immediately, while the slaughterer prays.

Clothing

The principles of Islamic dress are modesty and cleanliness, but what people actually wear is governed by the society in which they live. *Hijab* means 'cover' or 'veiling' – Muslim women are expected to be 'covered women', which they all accept – discussion arises only over the *extent* of the cover. Wearing revealing and sexually provocative clothing is regarded as pandering to the lowest instinct of the male (neither fair, nor sensible).

There are few rules for men's wear, except for pilgrims in *ihram*, and being covered from navel to knee for prayer. Men are not allowed to wear garments made of silk, unless they have a skin disorder that requires it. They should not wear jewellery other than a wedding ring, which should be made of silver and not gold.

Hijab

Islam requires women to cover their bodies from the neck to the wrist and foot. Most cover their heads, and some even cover their hands and faces, revealing only the eyes. The most extreme even cover their eyes and peep at the world through a see-through veil (one or two layers) or mesh.

Wearing the hijab.

The command in the Qur'an states that: '*Believing women should lower their gaze and guard their modesty; they should not display their ornaments except as is normal. They should draw their veils over their bosoms and not display their beauty except to their close male relatives.*' (Surah 24:30–31; the *surah* gives the precise list of these relatives.) Much ink has been spilt on the subject of the 'ornaments' referred to, but the majority of Muslims take it to mean that the private parts or outlines of the female body should definitely not be visible.

Those who wear a head-veil take this verse as the source of God's command to do so, although the verse emphasizes covering bosoms rather than heads – the Prophet once rebuked a female relative for being too informal by saying that once puberty is reached, a lady should only show 'this and this' – and he pointed at her face and hands.

Muslim men do not have the right to force *hijab* on a woman – doing so would break the Islamic injunction against coercion in religion. It is important to remember that people are not judged by their clothing, but for their characters and the quality of their lives. A fully covered woman might be proud, hard-hearted, cruel or selfish. A less-covered woman might have more natural modesty.

Work

Islam makes a clear difference between lawful and unlawful methods of earning a living. If your work hurts or abuses another person, or results in another's loss, it is *haram*. If it is fair and beneficial, then it is *halal*.

Any form of making money that involves dishonesty, deceit or fraud, bribery, robbery, hoarding in order to take advantage of hardship, exploitation, artificial creation of shortages, or anything to do with alcohol, gambling or lotteries, sexual degradation or immoral practices, is also forbidden to Muslims.

Employees have a duty to their employers, as well as to those they support, so should not cheat them in any way. Equally, employers should treat their employees with justice and kindness, and should pay them fairly without delay, make sure they are protected from danger in the workplace, and not exploit them or make them work unreasonable hours or in unreasonable conditions.

It is considered very important that a man *does* work (unless unable to do so through illness or other handicap), and does not stay idle or become a burden to others. Begging is strongly disapproved of, unless there is no alternative.

Collective responsibilities

Certain crafts and industries are seen as collective obligations (*fard kifaya*) – things essential to the community. These include education, medicine, science and technology, politics, community welfare, waste disposal, burial of the dead, and the clothing, utensil and agricultural industries (food and water). All productive resources (including unemployed manpower, unused land, and water or mineral resources) should be brought into use as far as possible, and never left idle or wasted.

Wealth and poverty

It is not forbidden for Muslims to become wealthy, and many Muslims are extremely wealthy, mainly through oil. But it is forbidden for wealthy Muslims to ignore the poor. Muslims know they really own nothing – everything in the universe belongs to God, so they do their best not to cling to material possessions. God stated, '*Those who are saved from their own greed shall be the successful*' (Surah 64:16). The Prophet knew how easy it was to be led astray by possessions, and commented: 'It is not poverty which I fear for you, but that you might begin to desire the world as others before you desired it, and it might destroy you as it destroyed them.' The lure of the world's luxuries and lusts that entice people from the right path is known as *dunya* ('the world').

Riba (exploitation)

Capitalizing on the misfortune or needs of others is called *riba*. Islam not only forbids trading in 'indebtedness' but actually forbids *any* unjustified advantage in trade dealings.

In Islam, money has to be used as a facility and not a commodity, or the owners of money gain an unfair advantage over the producers or traders. They could wait until the merchandise lost value (as in food crops and other perishables) and force merchants to sell at a low price; or they could buy up commodities and hoard them until they increase in value. Islam teaches that wealth should be in circulation and not hoarded for private gain.

Muslims must pay the *zakah*, and there are certain rules for business and banking – providers of funds can only share profits if they are willing to share the losses of the person who uses their money. This is known as *mudarabah*, the net profit of the trade being shared between the owner (*rab al-mal*) and the worker (*mudarib*) after it is realized at the end of the transaction.

Slavery

Kidnapping and enslaving law-abiding people is known as *hirabah*, and can incur the death penalty – a law that was previously given to the prophet Moses (Exodus 21:16). Today's slave trade largely involves the sex trade, people-smuggling, and domestic and child slavery. Muslims did not abolish the traditional type of slavery, in which people who were in debt might put themselves into service for an agreed term to work their way out of it – but the Prophet was told: *'Who will tell you what the ascent is? It is to free the slave'* (Surah 90.13). The act of buying a person out of debt and slavery was regarded as highly meritorious. It could also be used as a means of atonement for an enormous variety of wrongdoings, ranging from manslaughter (Surah 4.92) to making a futile oath (Surah 5.89).

Care of the environment

Muslims believe that the planet Earth holds a special place in the universe (meaning 'all that is') because of its laws of nature and life forms. Of these, humans have a special place, for they were created to care for the planet, develop and nurture it, and protect it. It is their duty to be a *khalifah*, a caretaker working for God (Surah 6:165). The Earth should not be neglected, exploited, wasted, or polluted. All the laws of nature are in delicate balance, according to God's will, and should not be put under threat.

want to know more?

• Wahiduddin Khan, *God-oriented Life*, Goodword Books, New Delhi, 1992
• R. Maqsood, *Living Islam*, Goodword Books, New Delhi, 1998

8 The history of Islam

Within a century of the Prophet's death Islam had spread east into the Persian empire, north into Byzantine territory, and west across North Africa and then into parts of Spain and Portugal. By the 14th century – mainly through the preaching and example of Sufi mystics – Islam had been spread to China, Central Asia, Turkey, sub-Saharan Africa, Indonesia and Malaya. Merchants and itinerant scholars also took their faith wherever they went. Now, around a fifth of the human race is Muslim.

The history of Islam

This chapter gives an outline of the most significant events and movements in the history of Islam, from the row over who should succeed the Prophet through to conflict in the Middle East in the late 20th and 21st century.

must know

The first four caliphs (known as 'ar-Rashidun', or 'Rightly Guided Caliphs') were the Prophet's closest friends, Abu Bakr (ruled 632-4), Umar (r. 634-46) and Uthman (r. 646-56), and Ali (r. 656-61).

Page 132: Detail of the Dome of the Rock, Jerusalem.

The Succession – Sunni and Shi'ite

Disagreement over who should succeed the Prophet as political and religious leader of the Muslim world commenced even before he was buried. Abu Bakr (whom the Prophet deputized to lead the prayers when he became ill) was elected, but many eminent Muslims felt strongly that the leadership had been promised to Ali.

Those who followed the Arab tradition of tribal consultation and election of the best elder came to be known as Sunnis, and those who maintained that the ruler, the 'caliph', must belong to the Prophet's actual dynastic line were called Shi'ites (from 'Shi'at Ali', or supporters of Ali). There were soon other sectarian splits.

Abu Bakr died only two years later; Umar's 10-year reign ended in his assassination in 644, and Uthman's 12-year rule met with increasing opposition, culminating in his assassination too. In 656 Ali was finally elected to rule both Sunni and Shi'a. He was opposed by Abu Bakr's daughter Aishah (the Prophet's widow – she survived her husband by 40 years) and Uthman's nephew Mu'awiyyah (who had been made Governor of Syria) for not bringing Uthman's killers to justice. She raised an army against Ali, which led to the first *fitna*

(Islamic civil war). Ali defeated her and advised her to spend the rest of her life teaching the faith but not involving herself in politics.

Ali remained Caliph, but had not been able to gain command over Mu'awiyyah's territory. Ali was also assassinated, and Mu'awiyyah became the first of the Umayyad caliphs.

The Muslim world remained a single political entity under the leadership of one caliph until the 9th century, but after that a series of caliphates were established in different places, each developing its own laws.

The spread of Islam

Jews and Christians were given a special status as 'People of the Book' (ahl al-kitab) and allowed religious autonomy. Anyone living under Muslim rule who did not accept Islam was expected to pay a tax, the jizyah. Muslims did not have to pay this since their own wealth was already taxed through the zakah.

But tensions were growing in the Muslim empire. The capital had switched from Makkah to Damascus in Syria. The Shi'ites opposed the Sunni leadership. Non-Arab converts demanded the same rights as Arabs. A move to establish a new leadership began in Persia and quickly spread throughout the rest of the empire, and in 750 the Umayyad dynasty was overthrown by the Abbasid (descendants of the Prophet's uncle Abbas), and the capital moved to Baghdad.

The Arab conquest of southern Spain ('al-Andalus') had begun in 710. The Umayyad Abdu'r Rahman I escaped the Abbasids in 750, fled to Spain, and had established his own caliphate there by 756.

must know

The leaders of the Shi'ites were not called caliphs but Imams (spiritual leaders – not to be confused with ordinary imams, the mosque prayer-leaders). Shi'ites believed that the Prophet gave special hidden teachings to Ali, which were then passed on to Ali's direct line. These Imams were revered as infallible. The 12th and last Imam disappeared in the 9th century, but is expected to return before Judgement Day.

Islamic rule had reached India in the 8th century when Muhammad ibn Qasim conquered Sindh (Pakistan), and Arab armies also conquered Afghanistan and other parts of India before moving north into central Asia, finally being stopped by the Chinese.

The Abbasid period was a period of great art and literature, an agricultural revolution and a boom time for commerce, industry and the sciences, especially in the reigns of the best three caliphs – al-Mansur (r. 754–75), Harun al-Rashid (r. 786–809) and al-Mamun (r. 809–13). The Shari'ah was codified, and the four leading religious schools of thought established. One great achievement was completion of the canonical collections of *hadiths*, and it also saw the rise of classical Sufism.

A group known as the Aghlabids ruled independently in North Africa, but fell to the Fatimids ('descendants of Fatimah') in 909, who went on to seize power in Egypt by *c.* 960, and built a new capital – 'al-Qahirah' (Cairo), meaning 'the victorious'. The Fatimids, a Shi'ite Isma'ili dynasty, ruled Egypt, North Africa, Sicily and Syria from 910 to 1171. In 1009 Caliph Hakim traumatized the Christian population of Jerusalem by ordering the destruction of the Church of the Holy Sepulchre. It was soon rebuilt, and pilgrimages were allowed, but for a time pilgrims risked capture and ill-treatment.

In Persia the Abbasids lost power to the Ghaznavids (975–1187), and then to the Seljuk Turks, who had migrated into Persia in 1055. Conquests continued under the Ghaznavids into the 12th century, when they were overtaken by the Ghurids in 1186. In 1206, one of the Ghurid generals, Qutb ud-din Aybak, conquered Delhi, and founded a succession of dynasties collectively known as the the Delhi Sultanate (1206–1526). These commanders were known as 'emirs', or sultans.

The Emirates, still recognizing the theoretical leadership of the caliphs, drifted into independence, and a brief revival of control was ended with the establishment of rival caliphates.

In Spain, by the end of the 10th century, the Umayyad caliphate of Abdu'l-Rahman III (912–61) paralleled that of Baghdad, but during the 11th century the kingdom broke down into over 40 independent principalities (*taifas*), which were much weaker than their Christian counterparts, and ended up paying tribute to them.

The Almoravid dynasty were Berber, from the Sahara, but extended their empire during the 11th century over present-day Morocco, the western Sahara, Mauritania, Gibraltar, Algeria, a great part of what is now Senegal and Mali in the south, and Spain and Portugal to the north in Europe.

The Almohads were also a Berber dynasty, founded in the 12th century, that conquered all northern Africa as far as Libya, together with al-Andalus.

The Turkish Seljuks ruled parts of Central Asia and the Middle East from the 11th to the 14th centuries. Their empire stretched from Anatolia to the Punjab in India, and it was largely their violence that spread the passion for the First Crusade.

The Crusades

The Byzantine Emperor, Alexius I Comnenus (1048–118), appealed to Pope Urban II for mercenaries to help him resist Muslim advances into the Byzantine Empire. However, in 1071, at the Battle of Manzikert, the Empire was defeated, leading to the loss of all of Asia Minor save the coastlands and the region around Constantinople. The Pope called for the First Crusade, to repel Muslim territorial expansion. Between the 11th and the 13th centuries, there were nine major crusades.

The warrior Saladin (1138–93), a Kurd born at Tikrit in Iraq, helped the decadent Fatimid caliph of Egypt repel the Crusaders. He became commander-in chief and vizier of Egypt. By 1171 he had united Egypt with the orthodox Abbasid caliphate, and in 1174 became Sultan of Egypt, the founder of the Ayyubid dynasty. In 1187 he invaded the Kingdom of

must know

Sufi Islam is a mystical tradition originating from the earliest days of Islam. Followers seek inner awareness of God rather than concentrating on details of practice. It emphasizes a quiet, simple life, renouncing worldly things, and meditation focused on attaining 'higher knowledge' and spirituality. Sufism gained impetus in the 10th century as a reaction against wealth and materialism, and has flourished ever since.

Jerusalem, defeated the Christians at Hittin in Galilee, and captured Jerusalem. In 1189 Pope Gregory VIII called for a new crusade to win Jerusalem back, and the Third Crusade was launched, led by Philip II of France, Richard I (the Lionheart) of England and Frederick I (Barbarossa). They failed to reclaim Jerusalem, but a peace was negotiated whereby unarmed Christian pilgrims would be allowed access.

The Mamluk Sultanate

The Mamluks (also spelled 'Mamelukes', from the Arabic for 'taken into possession' or 'owned') were slave-soldiers who served the caliphs and the Ayyubid sultans. They developed into a powerful military caste, defeated the Seventh Crusade and swept the Tartars (Mongols) out of Syria. The Mamluk commander Baybars ruled Egypt between 1260 and 1277.

The Mongols

In the 13th century Persia was overrun by the savage Mongols under Ghenghis Khan, who were determined to destroy Islam and brought the Abbasid era to a violent end. The Persian city of Isfahan fell to them by 1237, and Baghdad in 1258. The cities of Damascus and Aleppo fell shortly afterwards, in 1260. Central government came to an end and the Islamic empire splintered into regional kingdoms. Many Mongols then came to accept Islam.

Meanwhile, the Mamluks still ruled in Egypt, but after 1450 came economic decline, and in 1517 they were ousted by the Ottomans under Selim I and their territories were annexed.

Islam in the Maghreb

'Maghreb' means 'place of sunset' or 'the West' – the region of Africa north of the Sahara and west of the Nile (Libya, Tunisia, Algeria, Morocco and sometimes Mauretania). The first Arab dynasty in the western Maghreb was the Idrisid (788–985), named after Sultan Idris I (r. 788–791), who traced his ancestry back to Ali and Fatimah. His new kingdom was the first Shi'ite dynasty in the history of Islam. His son Idris II made Fez his capital, which became the focus for the Islamification of North Africa. In East Africa, Islam arrived mainly through trade, while in West Africa, the Sokoto caliphate was established in Nigeria in 1803. The Caliph, Shaykh Uthman Dan Fodio, was one of Africa's foremost Islamic religious teachers, writers and Islamic reformers. He wrote more than a hundred books, and encouraged literacy and scholarship, even for women. Several of his daughters emerged as scholars and writers, notably Nana Asma'u, who inspired a cadre of women teachers that travelled throughout the Caliphate educating women.

China and South-East Asia

Islam had progressed along the Silk Road to China while the Prophet still lived, and the first Chinese mosque was established in the city of Chang'an in 650.

Traders and Sufi missionaries took Islam to the islands of South-East Asia, and by 1292, when Marco Polo visited Sumatra, most of its population was Muslim, under the Sultanate of Aceh. The Sultanate of Malacca was founded in the Malay peninsula, and Islam soon spread to Borneo, Java, and the

Philippines. The Portuguese captured Malacca in 1511, and
Brunei became the chief South-Asian centre of Islam, with its
sultanate still in existence to this day.

The Gunpowder Empires

After *c.* 1400, the key military resource became gunpowder
weaponry – both large cannons that could demolish or defend a
walled city or fortress, and handguns that infantry could use to
destroy any force that did not have them. Armies were
reorganized, along with the societies that supported them.

The 15th and 16th centuries produced three major Muslim
empires – the Mughal in India, the Safavid in Iran, and the
Ottoman in the Middle East, Balkans and North Africa. They
were called 'Gunpowder Empires' because of their reliance on
this new method of warfare.

The Mughal Empire (1526–1857)

The founder of this dynasty, Babur (r. 1526–30) claimed descent
from Ghenghis Khan and Timur, and founded the Mughal
Empire when he overthrew the Delhi sultanate. The Mughals
ruled most of India for three centuries. North India and large
parts of the south had been ruled by Muslims for centuries, but
they were nevertheless in the minority and the Hindu elite were
still important. There was a great deal of intermarriage, and the
Mughal court was influenced by Persian culture as well. The only
way Muslims could accommodate this was by taking the Sufi
approach – that there was truth to be found in every religion.

Emperor Akbar ('Akbar the Great', 1556–1605) actually tried to
bring Muslim and Hindu traditions and practices together at his
court, despite the disquiet of Muslim scholars who felt this
universalism was against God's law.

Emperor Aurangzeb (1658–1707) favoured 'purifying' the court
of non-Muslim influences, and asserted the supremacy of
Muslims over the rest of the population, thus alienating the

Hindu aristocracy and military and undermining Mughal power. The Mughal dynasty was eventually dissolved by the British Empire after the Indian rebellion of 1857.

The Safavid Empire (1501–1736)

The Safavids (named from a Sufi order founded in the 14th century by Shaykh Safi, who claimed descent from Ali) were Iranian, from the borderland between Turkey and Iran. In 1501 their leader, Shah Isma'il, captured the Iranian capital Tabriz, suppressed the Sunni leaders and set up a Shi'ite religious college in every city. Under the Safavids, Iranian arts and crafts, architecture and literature flourished, but Iran became diplomatically isolated from Islamic countries that were not Shi'ite. The central government and royal court also became alienated from local Muslim communities who did not believe that the Safavids represented the true line of Ali.

The Ottoman Empire (1299–1924)

The Ottomans were a Turkish dynasty named after the 13th-century Anatolian warlord Ghazi Osman I, who assumed leadership of a key *beylik* in 1281, and by 1299 had declared an independent emirate and attacked the Byzantines.

By 1331 Osman's son Orhan had captured Nicaea, and in 1389 the Battle of Kosovo saw victory over the Serbs. Bayezid I took power in 1389, spread his empire into the Balkans and Anatolia, but was captured by the Mongol warlord Timur (Tamerlane, Tamburlaine) at Ankara in 1402. Timur split the territory up amongst Bayezid's sons, but in 1413 the youngest, Mehmed I, defeated his brothers and declared himself the new Ottoman Sultan.

In 1453, Mehmed II lay siege to Constantinople with large cannons, against which the Byzantines were unable to compete. With its capital conceded to the Ottomans and renamed Istanbul, the rest of the Byzantine Empire quickly disintegrated. The Ottomans also conquered the Balkan peninsula, thus acquiring a new Christian subject population and a tremendous amount of wealth and power. They began importing slaves from the Caucasus, and built up the most famous slave-recruited army in Islamic history (the 'Janissaries'). With this highly trained army, the Ottoman sultans made tremendous gains in south-eastern Europe.

In 1514 Selim I ended Safavid expansion, deposed the ruling Mamluks in Egypt, and in 1517 absorbed their territories into the Ottoman Empire. His successor Suleyman I (1494–1566) was the greatest Ottoman sultan, a conqueror who doubled the size of the empire.

Also known as Suleyman the Magnificent and al-Kanuni (the Law-maker), he recaptured Baghdad from Safavid control, advanced deep into Hungary, reached the gates of Vienna in 1529

The Jamia Masjid, Delhi.

must know

A reformer (*mujaddid*) is a person who tries to revive the authentic teachings of Islam without the encumbrance of social and cultural habits and ideas.

but was beaten back by an alliance of European forces, sowing the seeds of a bitter Ottoman-Hapsburg rivalry which lasted until the 20th century. After his reign, the Ottoman Empire fell into gradual decline.

Reformers

The Muslim world was falling into a state of decay compared to the dynamism of Europe. An acceptable formula was needed to reconcile Islam with the secularized West. Modernists sought to unburden Islam of all the unnecessary dogmas accumulated over the centuries, and face the challenge of the new world by being favourably disposed towards it. They insisted on:

• returning to the first principles of Islam through a new reading of the Qur'an which would show that the new sciences based on the principles of observation and experimentation were perfectly compatible with it;

• revitalizing *ijtihad* (independent reasoning) in Muslim thinking and practice;

• calling for the rejection of *taqlid* (imitation), the submission to the authority of classical jurists in interpreting the Qur'an and the Sunnah.

Saudi Arabia and Wahhabism

As Islamic regions fell increasingly under the sway of European imperial powers, many felt that their own weakness was due to a need for reform. In Central Arabia Muhammad ibn Abdu'l Wahhab (1703–92), for example, sought to return Islam to its original principles. His teachings were largely based on those of Ibn Taymiyyah (1263–1328), who believed that the Qur'an and the practice of the

Salafiyyah constituted an infallible guide to life –
he rejected any deviation from this as *bid'ah*
(innovation), and therefore forbidden. Abdu'l
Wahhab allied himself with the House of Saud in its
rise to power, and led several revolts against the
Ottoman empire.

However, in India, Abdu'l Wahhab's contemporary
Shah Walihullah (1703–62), took the view that the
Islamic code of life could only apply to all ages and all
peoples if it provided answers to the new problems
and situations. It was therefore the duty of Muslim
jurists to exercise *ijtihad* (their judgement) in re-
interpreting and making new provisions in law,
within the framework of the fundamentals of Shari'ah.

Sir Syed Ahmad Khan (1817–98) founded the
Scientific Society of Aligarh, the first scientific

**An interior view of the
Dome of the Rock,
Jerusalem.**

must know

For Muslims, the evolution debate is by no means settled. It can be accepted as a theory but not as a proven fact. See Harun Yahya, *The Evolution Deceit*, London, 1999.

association of its kind in India, modelled on the British Royal Society. He was in favour of showing that modern science and technology were in conformity with the articles of Islamic faith.

In Egypt, the outstanding figures in the Islamic Renaissance were Muhammad Abduh (1849–1905), in his early years a teacher at the al-Azhar university of Cairo, who later cooperated with Jamal al-Din al-Afghani (1839–97), founder and inspirer of the Pan-Islamic Movement. Al-Afghani was convinced that nothing but science and technology could eliminate economic and cultural backwardness. They called for a revitalization of Islam that would permit the absorption of modern science to bring reform to the Islamic world. They advocated:

• restoration of reason;
• no priesthood in Islam, or over-revered Imams;
• a return to individual *ijtihad*;
• democracy, and the practice of *Shura* (consultation);
• strong unity amongst all Muslim people from all nations.

Muhammad Abduh's rulings as the Chief Mufti of Egypt were influenced by the principle of public interest (*maslahah*). He observed: 'If a ruling has become the cause of harm which it did not cause before, then we must change it according to the prevailing conditions.'

When Modernist Muslims claim that the door of *ijtihad* has been closed, they are lamenting the loss of the spirit of inquiry that was demonstrated by classical Islamic civilization at its peak. Modernist Muslims see *ijtihad* as the desire for all forms of knowledge, not just religious and juristic, which needs to be revived to revitalize and restore Islamic civilization.

The Crimean War (1853–56) marked a major alliance between Christian and Islamic powers, for the Ottoman Empire joined forces with France and Britain against Russia. After this war, Muslim scholars became even more interested in European law and science. Some Islamic countries (such as Turkey and Egypt) attempted to separate Islam from the secular government, whereas others (such as Saudi Arabia) became ever more narrowly puritanical.

Reaction was split, and fundamentalist and modernist Islam were polarized. The fundamentalists, who developed from a tradition of militant (or at least strongly vocal) objection to any deviation from what was seen to be mainstream traditional Islam, particularly rejected the 'corruptions' of the West in its unIslamic attitudes towards sexual permissiveness, its use of alcohol and charging interest in banking. Symbolic attacks on banks, cinemas and newspapers were typical.

The 20th century

In Iran, a Constitutional Revolution took place between 1905 and 1911, which led to the restriction of the powers of the Shah (king) and the establishment of a parliament. However, the modernist and conservative blocks began to fight each other.

By the turn of the 20th century, the Ottoman Empire had seriously failed to keep pace with European technological and economic development. Turkey's decision to back Germany in World War I meant it shared the Central Powers' defeat, which led directly to the overthrow of the Ottomans in 1924

Sudanese man in prayer.

by Turkish nationalists led by Kemal Ataturk. Since then, there has been no major widely accepted claim to the caliphate.

With the defeat of the Ottomans the last Muslim empire collapsed, and with its destruction, its remnants were parcelled out as European protectorates. Lebanon and Syria ended up under the control of the French, who also occupied Morocco, Algeria and Tunisia at various times during the early part of the century. Italy had already taken control of Libya after the 1911–12 Italo-Turkish war, and the British took control of the areas that became Istanbul, Iraq, Palestine and Trans-Jordan.

With Islamic revival now seen as imperative by activists, in 1928 the Egyptian Hasan al-Banna (1906–49) founded the Muslim Brotherhood (al-Ikhwan al-Muslimun). One of the most pious and influential of Muslim revivalist organizations, it was also the key predecessor of the more militant Islamic fundamentalist groups of the late 20th century. Al-Banna was assassinated, probably by a government agent, in February 1949, when he was only 43 and at the height of his career.

Meanwhile, the discovery of oil and petroleum altered everything for the Middle East. German experts had reported plentiful supplies of oil in Iraq as early as 1871, and by 1907 it was said to be a veritable 'lake of petroleum'. Oil was also found in quantity in Iran, in 1908. The major Iraqi field at Kirkuk opened in 1927, in 1932 it was discovered in commercial quantities in Bahrain, and in Qatar in 1939. World War II temporarily halted production, but it soon began to flood out to the world market whose economies rapidly became dependent on it.

Meanwhile, Arab socialism (especially the Arab Socialist Ba'ath Party and the Nasserite Movement) were emerging as a stream of thought that played down the role of religion.

In 1947 the two nations of India and Pakistan were formed out of the former British Raj, and Pakistan was partitioned into Bengal and Punjab. (In 1971, after a bloody war of independence, the Bengal part of Pakistan became an independent state called Bangladesh).

In 1948 the British also established the State of Israel as a Jewish nation state, displacing many Palestinian people and creating enormous animosity in the Muslim world when agreed United Resolutions were not kept.

In Egypt, Sayyid Qutb (1906–66) became the leading intellectual of the Muslim Brotherhood in the 1950s and '60s. He is best known in the Muslim world for his work on the social and political role of Islam, his many inspirational writings including *Ma'alim fi'l Tariq* (*Milestones*), and his extensive commentary on the Qur'an. However, a visit to the United States spurred a reaction of intense dislike of the attitudes he saw and experienced, and he became much more radical. His revolutionary ideology of *takfir* (excommunication) influenced the new generation. After opposing the government of Jamal Abdul Nasser, he spent most of the rest of his life in prison, and was eventually tried and executed for treason. To this day, Qutb is considered to be a major source of insurrectionary ideology.

One of his students was Ayman Zawahiri, who went on to become a member of the Egyptian Islamic Jihad terror group and later a leading member of al-Qaeda.

must know

Suicide bombing is totally forbidden in Islam. According to mainstream belief, terrorists are not martyrs being put to death for their faith but people choosing to die as suicides and murderers of innocent civilians.

Along with Maulana Maududi, the founder of Jamaat-e-Islami (the revivalist movement in South Asia), Qutb nevertheless gave shape to the ideas and world view that have mobilized and motivated millions of Muslims from Malaysia to Michigan to strive to reintroduce Islamic practices in their lives and alter social and political institutions so that they reflect Islamic principles.

1967–present

Israel and its Arab neighbours have been hostile towards each other since 14 May 1948, when Israel became a nation in an area that Palestinian Arabs claim as their homeland. In the Six Day War (5–10 June 1967), pre-empting an imminent invasion by surrounding Arab states, Israel conquered the Sinai Peninsula, Gaza Strip, West Bank and Golan Heights, which became collectively known as the Occupied Territories.

Many in the Islamic world saw the loss of the Six Day War against Israel as the failure of socialism. It was at this point that fundamental and militant Islam began to fill the political vacuum created.

The Arab defeats in the Six Day War and the 1973 Arab-Israeli Wars triggered an oil crisis, with the Arab world imposing an oil embargo against the United States and Western Europe. Since then, the Western economy has been largely held hostage to oil interests and production.

In 1979 there was an Islamic Revolution in Iran in support of the Shi'ite cleric Ayatollah Ruhollah Khomeini (1902–89), who had conducted a preaching mission using tape-cassettes during a 20-year imprisonment and exile. His return to Iran triggered the overthrow of the Shah and a popular referendum created a theocratic Islamic Republic. At the same time, the US, USSR and most of the Arab governments feared that their dominance in the region was challenged by the new Islamic ideology, so they encouraged and supported Saddam Hussein to invade Iran, which resulted in the 10-year Iran-Iraq War. His subsequent invasion of Kuwait brought US troops into Saudi Arabia to repel him, and protect oil interests.

In recent years moderate Islam has suffered as extremist groups have proliferated all over the world, voicing their dislike of concepts such as democracy and modernity – which are usually associated with the imposition of Western secular beliefs and values, seen as atheism, immorality and materialism.

The vast majority of Muslims reject extremism and regard it as contrary to the teaching of the Qur'an, the Prophet and the spirit of Islam. They remain 'traditional' (largely apolitical and accomodationist), which therefore makes them vulnerable to criticism from radical activists, who accuse them of being complicit in the crimes of secular states, as opposed to promoting the creation of 'the Islamic state' (or 'Islamization' of the existing nation-state).

On 11 September 2001, the twin towers of the World Trade Centre in New York were demolished by hijacked planes, leading to the 'campaign against terror' (seen by many as an excuse to control the oil reserves) concentrating on Osama bin Laden and the al-Qaeda organization, the war in Afghanistan against the extreme Taliban movement, and a second campaign in Iraq that led to Saddam Hussein's capture and execution.

want to know more?

• **Bloom and Blair**, *Islam: A Thousand Years of Faith and Power*, 2000
• **Esposito, John**, *Oxford History of Islam*, Oxford University Press, 2000
• **Jorgen Nielsen**, *Towards a European Islam*, London, 1999
• **Nasr, Seyyed Hossein**, *Islam: Religion, History and Civilization*, New York, 2003
• **Karen Armstrong**, *Islam, A Short History*, 2000

9 Islamic heritage

As Islam has spread throughout the world it has influenced and been influenced by every culture it touched. The orthodox objection to portraying the human form (or in some cases, any life form) discouraged painting and sculpture, but Muslim artisans and craftsmen soon gained such a reputation that their products were keenly sought all over the known world.

Islamic heritage

In this chapter you will be introduced to the Islamic heritage of architecture, arts and crafts, textiles, carpets, woodwork, tiles and portable objects in ceramic, precious metals and alloys, ivory and rock crystal, to music, dance and literature.

Islamic architecture

Islamic architecture excels in three main categories (apart from the mosque – see Chapter 5). These are the palace, the fortress/castle and the tomb/shrine. The finest architectural monuments are in Spain, Egypt, Iraq, Iran and the Indo-Pakistan sub-continent.

Palaces and Mausoleums

After the death of the Prophet, the first caliphs had no desire for luxury living. However, it did not take long for rulers to build themselves sumptuous palaces that offered limitless scope for artists, architects and artisans to ply their skills.

As it was dangerous to be a ruler, their palaces were often built like fortresses. They would include *hammams* (bath-houses), kitchens, dining rooms, and quarters for the family and servants. Soldiers were housed outside.

Palaces incorporated expensive materials (such as marble), and were lavishly gilded and decorated with beautiful paintings, tiles, carpets and chandeliers, sometimes even with walls inlaid with precious gems.

The Mughal period in India was particularly noted for its fine architecture. The Taj Mahal was built by 20,000 craftsmen, and is one of the finest buildings

must know

Some of the most beautiful Islamic buildings were built to honour the dead. A famous example is the Taj Mahal, built by Mughal Emperor Shah Jahan for his wife Mumtaz. He was said to have planned a black mausoleum for himself. It does exist – as a dark reflection in the pool of his recently restored Moonlight Garden.

Page 152: Detail of decorative tiles at Isfahan, Iran.

must know

For an excellent virtual tour of the Taj Mahal, linked to the World Heritage site, see www.taj-mahal.net

Fretwork passageway and arches, Malaysia.

in the world. The extensive use of precious stones as inlay and the vast quantity of white marble required nearly bankrupted the Empire.

In the 13th century the last Muslim dynasty of Spain made Granada its capital, and the Alhambra became the royal city; its famous palace was unsurpassed for the exquisite detail of its marble pillars and arches, its fretted ceilings and the veil-like transparency of its filigree work in stucco. It is also famous for its gardens.

From the 13th century, Persia developed its own style, distinguished for its refinement and delicacy, furthering ornamentation, arabesque and glazed coloured tiles.

In the 15th century the Ottoman emperor, Suleyman the Magnificent, built the Topkapi Palace and the Suleymaniya Mosque. The Topkapi was a city-palace for nearly 400 years, home to 25 sultans.

Above: The Castle Krak des Chevaliers, Syria, which was originally Kurdish.

Castles and forts

As Islam spread, and territories from Spain to India came under its rule, it met with opposition from Byzantine Christians, and Muslims battled each other for control of the Empire and the religious authority as successor to Muhammad. Castles and fortresses were therefore essential. Characteristic features included towers, high walls with crenellations and slit windows, and massive gates, often with drawbridges, moats and a portcullis. A chain of ruined fortresses can still be seen en route to Jerusalem.

Islamic architecture now holds its place in the modern world with many wonderful and exciting projects. Oil has given many Muslims vast wealth, and luxury projects are springing up to cater for travel, business, Islamic banking, educational institutions, airports, and so on. The leading architects include Hassan Fat'hi, Rifat Chadirji, Basil al-Bayyati and Abdel Wahed el-Waki.

Literature and learning

By the 12th century *madrassahs* (somewhat similar to medieval universities) were established all over the Muslim world offering courses in philosophy, mathematics, astronomy and medicine, as well as Islamic jurisprudence. Most were privately endowed by rich benefactors, and sometimes the founding scholar would be buried at the school, in a mausoleum.

The Abbasid caliph Mansur founded a translation department to bring classical and scientific works into Arabic, thus making the philosophical, mathematical and scientific works of Greek scholars available to the public.

Cairo housed one of the largest libraries in the world, occupying 40 chambers in the imperial palace, a collection of between 200,000 and 600,000 volumes, including 18,000 books of philosophy and 24,000 Qur'ans.

The intellectual life of the Islamic world was nearly wiped out by the destruction of the Mongol hordes. Ghenghis Khan remorselessly burned major works accumulated over the centuries. In 1258, Hulagu destroyed Baghdad, and the ink from the millions of books he threw into the River Tigris literally made the water run black.

Muslims view Arabic as the sacred language, and the writing of the Word of God as the most venerated form of art, with expert calligraphers much held in honour. Calligraphy was thought of as an expression of the artist's spiritual state, and that purity of writing came from a pure heart. Arabic calligraphy is associated with geometric Islamic art (arabesque) on the walls and ceilings of mosques as well as on the page.

did you know?

At a time when Westerners believed the Earth was flat, the Cairo Palace collection included a globe made by Ptolemy that was 2,250 years old.

must know

The al-Azhar University of Cairo is the biggest university of the Islamic world, with over 10,000 students. It opened for service in 972, and was the only great Muslim institution left in the world after the Mongol devastations.

Calligraphers were trained from a young age, sometimes from childhood. The great calligraphers could write perfectly even without the proper tools and materials, and many learned to write equally well with both hands, in case one should be lost.

The scripts

Kufic script was the dominant early script, developed in Kufah towards the end of the 7th century. It is a thick, bold, monumental style, and was used chiefly for inscriptions in stone and metal. It is angular, much wider than it is high, with low verticals and extended horizontal strokes, easy to carve in walls and wood, and often used on oblong surfaces. It was the main script used to copy the Qur'an for 300 years. Later Kufic writing developed many little decorative features (called *serifs*).

Calligraphy also has a figurative aspect when anthropomorphic or zoomorphic figures are produced by interweaving written words. They are related to mysticism and have been popular with many leading calligraphers in Turkey, Persia/Iran and India from the 17th century onward.

Hassan Massoudy (b. Iraq, 1944) is one of the world's most important contemporary calligraphers.

Poetry and drama

Like most faiths, Islam inspired poetry and drama (the Shi'ite plays commemorating the martyrdom of Husayn at Karbala are a key example). Poetry was highly valued and there were famous competitions. Talented poets could earn a good living by travelling from city to city to recite poetry to wealthy hosts, or even make money on the streets, in the market-

place and in tea or coffee houses (like the trouba-
dours or travelling singing storytellers of Europe).
Sufis used to gather for regular recitations of the
works of their *shaykhs*.

There were five main types of poetry:
• the *qasida* – a poem with lines all ending with the
same rhyme;
• the *ghazel* – a love-poem with from 5 to 20 rhyming
couplets (religious or secular);
• the *qitah* – used for satire, jokes, riddles and word
games;
• the *manavi* – originating in Persia, used to tell a
long story by stringing together thousands of
rhyming couplets;
• the *ruba'i* – another Persian form, with quatrains in
which the first, second and fourth lines rhyme. The
most famous example is the *Rubaiyat of Omar
Khayyam*.

Travelogues

Travel books (*rihla*) were a type of Arabic literature
that flowered in North Africa between the 12th and
14th centuries. The best known examples tell of
journeys from North Africa to Makkah for Hajj. They
entertained and informed the readers with rich
descriptions of the public monuments, mosques,
religious personalities, governments, customs, and
curiosities of the cities of the Islamic world.

The main reason why the achievements of
Muslims are not generally known was because the
largest collections of literary and artistic treasures
accumulated during the first five centuries of Islamic
rule perished during the times when they were

defeated – for example, the manuscripts of Baghdad were destroyed by Hulagu Khan.

Stories

The *Maqamat* are the most popular expression of the Arabic spirit. These were stories written in rhymes, the heroes usually being common people who were caught up in many entertaining adventures.

The *Thousand and One Nights* (*Alf Laylah wa Laylah*) is one Arabic work that has become truly popular in the West. The first compilation was made in Iraq in the 10th century by al-Jahshiyari who added tales from local storytellers to an old Persian work, *Hazar Afsana* (the 'thousand tales'), which in turn contained some stories of Indian origin. The framework is the storytelling talent of Princess Scheherazade, the newest wife of King Shahrayar (who kills all his wives after their wedding night). She saves herself with her endless supply of bedtime stories, which included the tales of Aladdin, Ali Baba and the Forty Thieves, Sinbad the Sailor, and many more.

Islamic art

Muslims have always patronized and participated in the propagation of fine arts. Islam was spreading at a time when the Christian Church was developing wonderful art and architecture in the key cities around the world – carved stonework, mosaics, statues, icons, gilded wood, painted murals, stained glass, embroidery, vestments, gold and silver crosses and chalices. Muslims had a problem, however, because they disagree on the permissibility of art, especially the depiction of living things.

Some maintain there should be no pictures or statues of any living things at all; some forbid pictures and statues of human beings or angels; some accept pictures because they are two-dimensional and only object to three-dimensional statues (Graeco/Roman/Christian art was full of statues). Although the Qur'an, like the Bible, prohibits the making of idols and bowing down to them' (i.e. in worship), it does not actually forbid representations of humans, animals or birds – so other Muslims accept paintings that are not part of religious art, such as illustrations for books, or portraits of national leaders. All agree that there should never be paintings or statues in a mosque.

Paintings and fine art

No ancient canvases or wood-panel paintings of Islamic origin have been found. However, Orthodox hostility to representative art proved only a temporary setback. The desert castles in Jordan reveal that the Umayyad caliphs were very content to decorate their private apartments with frescoes depicting human figures, even nude figures of dancing girls.

Excavations have uncovered fragmented wall paintings of a secular nature, and Muslims are responsible for a great number of small paintings on paper which served as book illustrations and miniatures. Some were religious, and even included paintings of the prophets.

The Sultans of Ottoman Turkey, Safavid Persia and Mughal India actually encouraged paintings as court art. Some commissioned illustrated books to recount the life of Muhammad and previous prophets.

must know

The Prophet's wife Aishah once decorated a door-curtain or wall-hanging with embroidered birds, and the Prophet asked her to remove it, since it distracted him from his prayers. She was allowed to make it into cushions instead. Once he said that 'angels will not enter a house in which there are statues'.

In the 10th century the Fatimid rulers of Egypt became patrons of illuminated manuscripts and miniatures (often accompanying translations of Greek scientific works into Arabic), painted in brilliant colours, sometimes against backgrounds of gold. Naturalistic treatment of animals was combined with elaborate and intricate designs. Persian miniature painting developed into a very sophisticated art in which figures in court scenes, hunts and battles move against panoramic backgrounds.

After the Mongol conquests of central Asia, Persia and China (c. 1258), a greater naturalism developed, inspired by Chinese landscape painting, which utilized light, feathery brushstrokes and delicate tints, and attempted to render backgrounds in three dimensions.

The 14th-century Shiraz school favoured brilliant colours, a love of gorgeous landscapes, birds and flowers, and faces and figures with rounded contours, narrow eyes and characteristic sideways glances.

The Ottoman sultans were great patrons of the arts, and 15th-century Turkish painting was characterized by forcefulness and realism. Some painters began to sign their work, the most famous being Bihzad (1440–1514), with his interest in character and the affairs of everyday life.

Film

Film is, of course, a modern art. Oral and written descriptions of the Prophet have always been considered quite acceptable, but visual depictions have been disputed, therefore very few films have featured the Prophet. In Egypt in 1926, when a film was proposed about the grandeur of the early days of Islam, the al-Azhar University alerted Egyptian public opinion, and published a *fatwa* stipulating that Islam categorically forbade the representation of the Prophet and his companions on the screen. King Fu'ad threatened to exile the chief actor if he went ahead.

More recently, others have taken a more relaxed view. A *fatwa* of the Iraqi Shi'ite Ali al-Sistani suggested that it *was* permissible to depict the Prophet, even in TV and movies, so long as the portrayal did not disrespect him. In 1977, Anthony Quinn starred in the key role of the Prophet's uncle Hamzah in a famous Muslim film, *The Message*, but it never directly showed the Prophet himself.

A venture into the world of cartoons is *Muhammad: The Last Prophet*, an animated retelling of the events surrounding the birth of Islam, using two techniques to get round the problem of never showing the Prophet himself – it is partly filmed from the Prophet's own point of view, and the Prophet is also provided with a kind of secular stand-in, a follower who recounts the story of Islam to his young daughter. It was due to open in the USA in 2002 but was shelved after the 9/11 attacks for fear of anti-Muslim sentiment. It was finally released in 2004.

Music and dance

Islam has a long tradition of music and song used as a medium to express joy in the faith. There is no 'typical' Muslim music, for there are different styles from Africa, to Uzbekistan, to Bosnia and Turkey, to Spain, to India. Arabs enjoy music, from the lullaby to the elegy. Under the Abbasids, music was studied as a science, a branch of mathematics.

Seville became a great centre of music in the 11th century and was famous for the manufacture of musical instruments. Europe learnt Arabic music through Spain, while the Chinese acquired it from Baghdad.

In 10th-century Persia, Isfahani's celebrated musical work, the *Great Book of Songs*, ran into 21 volumes. Abu Nasr Farabi (d. 950), one of the greatest musical theorists the Muslim world produced, included among his books the *Grand Book on Music (Kitab Mausiqal Kabir)*, and *Styles in Music*, on the classification of rhythm. Farabi was also an outstanding practical musician of his

must know

Al-Khwarizmi, the greatest mathematician of the Islamic world, wrote *The Key of Sciences*, in which he discussed the theory of music. His views were translated by Adelard of Bath in the 12th century.

time and his flute-playing could make people break into laughter or burst into tears.

However, it is also true that music is disapproved of, if not forbidden, by some Muslims. In fact, there is a full range of opinions on the subject.

• Some Muslims believe that only vocal music is permissible, and that instruments are totally forbidden.

• Some allow traditional instruments such as drums and the various types of lute.

• Others feel that instruments are lawful so long as they are used for permissible kinds of music – they would accept folk and classical music, but not pop music with sexual lyrics or provocative rhythms.

• Many Muslims do not categorize specifically religious music as music but as 'devotion' – thus calling the *adhan*, recitation of the Qur'an, religious songs and meditations are all allowed.

• Some maintain that music and dance are uplifting and can be forms of worship, and a means to draw people closer to God.

There is no ban on music mentioned in the Qur'an, therefore it falls into the category of that which is left to the conscience of the individual. Those who try to ban music do it solely on the strength of two *hadiths* about signs that will foreshadow the end of the world. The debate has continued for centuries and the community remains divided on the issue.

Music, chanting, dance, twirling and poetry are all *celebrated* in such cultures as Turkey and Persia within the Sufi tradition, an attitude opposed by fundamentalists. Sufi music has a hypnotic quality – sometimes musical prayer ceremonies last all night, and coffee is drunk at regular intervals to keep the participants going.

Islamic music

Islamic music is always religious music sung or played in public services or private devotions. Much of it is recitation without any accompaniment by musical instruments, as in the *adhan*, the prayers and Qur'an recitations performed by professionals. One of the joys of Arab music is the use of quarter-tones. The Western piano has eight white keys and five black keys per octave – 13 notes. In Arabic classical music an octave may have 17, 19 or even 24 notes, which can be produced vocally or on string instruments, but not on pianos since they come 'in between' the keys.

Devotional songs are called *nasheed*, performed by individuals or more usually groups. Some use only voice and percussion instruments, which are considered *halal*. Others do add instruments. In Turkey and other parts of the Middle-East, Sufi musicians often use long-necked lutes called *tanbur*, instruments that originated around 3000 BCE, some played with plectrum and some with bow.

Similar instruments are the *rubab* (a plucked lute – the national Afghan instrument), Turkish *saz* or *baglama*, the Bulgarian *tambura*, the Iranian *setar* and the Iraqi *buzuq*. A favourite in the Asian subcontinent is the hand-pumped Indian harmonium (*armonia*).

Sufi music and chanting is usually called *dhikr* (or *zikr*), meaning 'remembrance of God'. Best known in the West are the chanting and whirling dancing of the Mevlevi dervishes of Turkey, who may these days

must know

Moorish Spain was a centre for the manufacture of musical instruments, especially the guitar (Ar. *al-qitara*).

The Islamic singing group Raihan.

perform for public enjoyment with a whole ensemble of instruments – in religious mood, but not an actual religious service. Concerts or gatherings for sacred songs are called *Mehfil-e-Sama*. Another Sufi order that uses music is the Chishti, which regards music as *qaza-yeh ruh* ('food for the soul'), a form of spiritual nourishment. *Sikiri* (from '*dhikr*') is performed by the Qadiriyya Sufi orders in East and Southern Africa (Tanzania, Mozambique, Malawi, Zimbabwe and South Africa).

In India and Pakistan religious music is called *qawwali*. Its aim is to enhance the remembrance of Allah, and it tends to begin gently and build steadily to a very high energy level in order to induce hypnotic states both among the musicians and the audience. Typical programmes include songs in praise of Allah, the Prophet, the teachers of the Sufi order, and *ghazals* ('songs of yearning') which use the language of romantic love to express the soul's longing for the divine.

Shi'ite Sufis use music for public religious celebrations. This includes *mawlid* music, performed for the birthday of the Prophet; *ta'zieh* music for the passion plays depicting the martyrdom of Imam Husayn at Karbala; and *ashura* music, performed during the Muharram mourning period.

Dance

As with music, there is difference of opinion. Some Muslims regard all dancing as sinful, while others will allow folk-dancing between separate groups of men or women (but not mixed sex). Many folk dances celebrated the achievements of warriors (such as sword dances), the agricultural calendar or rites of passage. In many Muslim societies women-only gatherings sing and dance before weddings.

Arab and North African Muslims often perform line-dancing, usually with swords, on joyful occasions, to welcome visitors (President Bush was recently treated to the spectacle in Bahrain), or as part of Sufi gatherings. The Prophet actually once sanctioned a group of Abyssinian dancers with swords to perform in his mosque.

The worry is that mixed dancing, touching during dancing, revealing clothing, and suggestive movements all encourage illicit sexual urges (Western dancing is thought far too sexual). Some

The whirling dervishes of Qonya.

must know

Arabs invented the *ghazal* or love song. The great Sufi Shaykh al-Ghazali (1059–1111) wrote in his treatise on music that listening to it induced a state of ecstasy.

Muslims would perhaps allow watching a professional dancer, but puritans would hardly approve 'ballroom' dancing in scanty costumes, and even classical ballet, where ballerinas lift their legs above their heads, is considered outrageous. Belly dancing, often regarded by non-Muslims as a part of Muslim culture, is not Muslim at all, and would not be watched by devout Muslims. Neither would the wet-blouse dancing of Hindu Bollywood films.

One form of Sufi dance popular in Turkey was the Whirling Dervishes' ritual called '*sema*' – whirling in a religious trance. Today it has become more commercialized and is presented before audiences, but its original purpose was to bring the dancer in closer contact with God, much like a meditation.

Many Muslims felt these rituals went against the teachings of Islam. One of the first measures of the strict Wahhabi sect when they seized control of Saudi Arabia in the early 20th century was to destroy the tombs of the Sufi masters and outlaw the practice of venerating 'dead' saints.

Islamic crafts

The secular art of many Islamic rulers reflected their taste for luxurious adornment and furnishings, symbols of their power and position. They surr-ounded themselves with sumptuous objects of glass, precious metals, and ivory, and lived in palaces richly decorated with wall paintings and stucco reliefs. Paintings, metalwork, ceramics, and wood and ivory carvings illustrated royal wealth and status in scenes of courtly life, feasting and hunting.

Geometric motifs were popular with Islamic artists and designers in all parts of the world for decorating almost every surface, whether walls or floors, pots or lamps, book covers or textiles.

Textiles and fabrics

Islamic textiles were famous throughout the world, serving as both clothing and household furnishings. Fine textiles were luxury goods, dignifying wealth and social status. Rich fabrics in a riot of colours, often incorporating gold and silver-wrapped threads, were characteristically distributed by rulers to members of the court. Their designs included calligraphy and complex arabesques.Few examples survived from the earliest Islamic period, however – not so much because they were fragile, but because of their value! Fabrics were cut down and re-used over and over again, until they literally wore out.

In the Mughal era, Muslim India was famed as a source of fine textiles. Kashmir became known for its shawls and Golconda for its chintzes.

Wood and ivory

Wooden fittings for architecture were particularly important where there were rich resources of timber. Gujarat was famous for its carved wood and its overlaid mother-of-pearl wares. The *kundekari* technique, widely used throughout the Islamic world by the 12th century, was a tongue-and-groove technique in which octagonal, stellate and lozenge-shaped panels carved with arabesque decoration were joined without pins or glue in grooved frames.

Some of the best woodwork can be found in Egypt, where wood was rare and costly. Carved wood was used for pulpits, screens, lattices over windows, valuable storage boxes, room dividers and all types of

must know

The English names of many fabrics derive from Arabic: cotton (*al-qutn*), mohair (*mukhayyar*, a type of haircloth), seersucker (which originates from *shir-o-shakkar* meaning 'milk and sugar'), damask (from Damascus – *dimashk*), and gauze from Gaza. Muslin was derived from *mussolina*, a cotton fabric supplied to Italy from Mosul, and special fine silken fabric (*baldachin*) was supplied by Baghdad.

Wooden screen, Morocco.

furniture. Floral designs and engraving of letters in wood and ivory works were common features.

The Ottoman court was famous for its luxury wooden objects – furniture and fittings, often inlaid with precious materials such as ivory, ebony, silver, gold, mother-of-pearl and tortoiseshell. Key items included elaborate manuscript boxes, Qur'an stands, storage boxes, backgammon sets and chessboards.

Córdoba, capital of Muslim Spain, was a great centre of ivory work, and had a famous school of ivory carving in the 10th century that produced beautiful caskets and boxes. One of the finest is a cylindrical casket kept in the Museo Arguelogico at

Madrid, presented as a gift by Caliph Hakam II to his wife in 964.

Glass

Islam has a fine heritage of glasswork, especially chandeliers and stained glass. The industry thrived in Syria particularly, and the process of enamelling and gilding glass was perfected by the craftsmen of Tyre. Glassware manufactured in Antioch, Aleppo and Damascus included lamps, lamp shades and vessels of exceptionally beautiful designs, and fetched a high price in medieval Europe.

Muslims also made glass bottles, jars, plates and bowls, drinking vessels and flasks with handles, reviving the ancient Egyptian technique of marvered and combed glass – where white glass thread was trailed round an existing glass object, then marvered (or pressed) into the darker glass beneath. It was then combed, producing a distinctive feathery pattern.

The Palestinian glass from Hebron is famous for its unique colours – rich deep blue, turquoise, gold and dark green. It can be seen in the stained-glass windows of the Ibrahimi mosque in Hebron or the Dome of the Rock in Jerusalem.

The Crusaders were said to have brought their techniques and colouring secrets back to the West when they returned home, to be used in the many great cathedrals and churches built in that period. Currently, there are 23 glass factories in Hebron, employing 300 workers.

Metalwork

Muslim artisans specialized in brass and bronze, often luxuriously inlaid with gold, silver and

must know

China was famous for its use of blue and white, but the typical blue was an innovation of Muslim potters, and even in China it was known as 'Muhammedan Blue'.

Turkish tiles in Muhammedan blue.

copper, and decorated with arabesques, inscriptions and stylized plant forms. Gilded silver was a favourite. Gold and silver objects usually do not survive, since they are melted down in times of need and reused. The numerous bronze and brass vessels and utensils illustrate the high degree of skill attained.

The technique of inlaying bronze or brass with precious metals predated Islam, and soon artisans were covering large areas of the base metal surface with decoration inlaid in copper and silver, gold and silver, or silver alone, producing a cheaper range of wares than those made of solid precious metals.

One important Islamic metalwork artifact was the astrolabe, designed to measure the altitude of the stars, sun or moon, and establish various data without resorting to calculations or formulae. The Muslim prayer-times were astronomically determined.

Metalworkers were also highly skilled in making jewellery, an industry that flourished in the Abbasid period.

Ceramics

Interiors and sometimes exteriors of the buildings were extensively decorated with off-set brick, stucco, *ablaq* (striping) or tile.

As far back as the 8th century potters working in what is now Iraq developed a mysterious process called 'lustre'. This was described as an 'extraordinary metallic sheen, which rivals even precious metals in its effects, all but turning objects of clay to gold'. Islam prohibited the use of gold and silver vessels, but lustre provided a similar effect in a cheaper and acceptable way. The technique involved preparing pigments by mixing silver or copper oxides with an earthy vehicle such as sulphur or ochre, and then vinegar or grape juice were added as medium. This pigment was then painted onto the glassy surface of a previously glazed and fired object. The vessel was then fired for a second time in a reducing kiln, so that the oxygen was drawn out of the metal oxides, and then the ochre was rubbed away to reveal a dazzling metallic lustre varying from rich gold to a deep red-brown. It was a costly and time-consuming process, only for luxury wares.

Potters also developed (after the 13th century) a method of polychrome painted-ware called *minai* (from the Persian word for enamel). They usually depicted lively scenes, with horsemen, princes and courtiers, entertainers, musicians and dancers (all in bright costumes).

The same techniques were utilized in tile-making, and in that industry the Muslims were unsurpassed. Tiles decorate the inside and outside of mosques, palaces and homes. They, too, bore calligraphy, designs and paintings. In Iran, where building material was dun brick, important monuments were gloriously embellished with vivid tiles. The most complicated and time-consuming was mosaic faience, where floral and other designs were cut from different coloured glazed tiles and assembled like a mosaic and fixed with mortar.

Stucco was originally applied directly to cover an unattractive surface, such as clay brick (or adobe), cinder block or stone. Applied wet, it sets hard in 48 hours. In wood-framed buildings, stucco was applied over wood laths. It was soon exploited for its decorative effects as it provided a ground for applied decoration – it can be moulded, carved, and painted in many different ways. For fine stuccowork, the wet plaster would be dusted with powdered talc and gypsum and then rubbed to give a high gloss. For painted surfaces, the plaster would be soaked with linseed oil and coated with sandarac oil.

Muqarnas is the Arabic word for a stalactite vault, an ornamental feature unique to Islamic architecture, developed around the middle of the 10th century in both north-eastern Iran and central North Africa. *Muqarnas* are small pointed niches stacked in tiers, projecting beyond those below, constructed in brick, stone, stucco or wood. They were often used to provide the transition between a square base and a dome to create a concave semi-vault above an entrance, or a cornice along the perimeters of a ceiling or beneath a balcony.

The arabesque is an elaborate application of repeating geometric forms that often derive from the forms of plants, shapes and sometimes animals (specifically birds). These forms constituted an infinite pattern that extended beyond the visible material world, symbolizing the infinite nature of creation. The intricate pattern evolved into Islamic art's most distinctive motif, and adorned even the most humble of objects as well as the walls of mosques and Muslim homes and buildings.

Carpets

Carpet-making has long been a tradition among the Bedouin tribes of Arabia, Persia and Anatolia. For the nomad, rugs were both decorative and utilitarian, serving as tents, floor coverings, curtains for privacy, and many other useful items such as saddlebags, blankets and saddle covers. The Muslim carpet has long been a luxury commodity, however, sought by textile museums, rich collectors and wealthy merchants all over the world.

The oriental rug has become valued throughout the world as the aristocrat of carpets. To a large degree, the precision of the design depends on how tightly the rug has been knotted and how short the pile has been cut. The rug's density, or number of knots per square inch, can be a useful indicator of the fineness and durability of the rug (the more knots the better). A superb oriental rug may have more than 500 to 1000 knots per square inch – each knot is tied by hand, and skilful artisans can tie about 15 knots a minute (this means it would take more than two months to weave a 3-metre by 2-metre carpet). Artisans work together from a chart, which shows the number of knots to be tied in each colour.

Beautiful colours could be produced from madder, a common plant that grows wild in Persia. Its roots gave various shades of red and pink, and when combined with a mixture of milk and fermented grape juice, yielded a violet dye. The bright red cochineal insect also provided red dye, as did the kermes insect that lives in the bark of oak trees.

Most rugs are made from wool, goat's or camel's hair, cotton and silk. The finest wool is thought to come from Kurdistan. Wool from Khorasan and Kirman is famous for its fine, velvety texture, while wool from the Caucasus and Central Asia is strong and lustrous.

want to know more?

• George Michell (ed.), et al, *Architecture of the Islamic World*, 1995
• Henri Stierlin, Anne Stierlin (photographer), *Islam: early architecture from Baghdad to Jerusalem and Cordoba*, 1996
• Cynthia Davidson (ed.), *Legacies for the future: contemporary architecture in Islamic societies*, 1999
• Henri Stierlin, Anne Stierlin (photographer), *Splendours of an Islamic World*, 1997
• *Islamic Architecture of Isfahan*: www.isfahan.org.uk
• For more images by Peter Sanders (responsible for most of the pictures in this book) see: www.peter sanders.co.uk
• *Tour of Islamic Architectural Sites* – far and away the best collection of images of Islamic architecture on the web. www.uga.edu/ islam/IslArt.html
• *See also* www.islamic architecture.org
• *And* www.albab.com/ arab/visual/architecture. htm

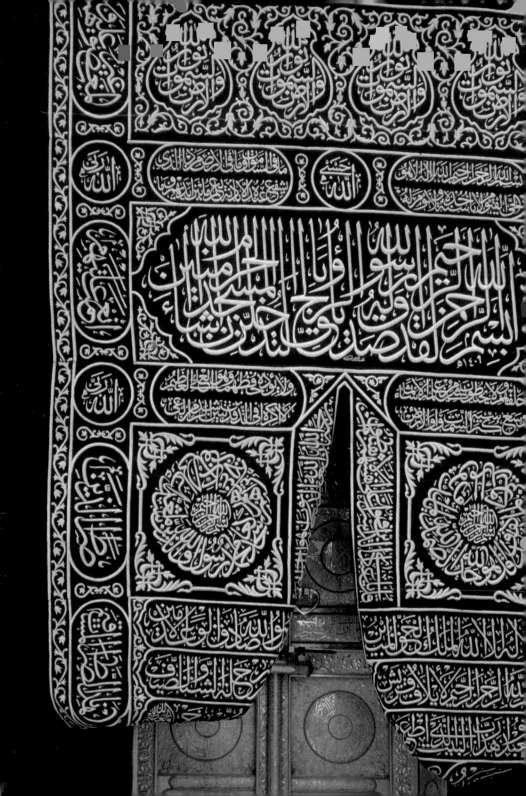

10 Issues for today

Today, Islam is the fastest-growing religion in the world, partly through conversions and partly through population growth. This is particularly true of the West, Europe and the Americas, where Islam is still 'new'. Through education, travel and contact, people are discovering that terrorism, fundamentalism, brutality and abuse of women and children are not at all representative of Islam, even though some Muslim men (just like some non-Muslim men) are guilty of them. This chapter considers the concerns that preoccupy Muslims as they encounter new cultures and new opportunities presented by today's 'global village'.

Issues for today

The growth of political Islam in the last century, the dominance of ultra-conservative Islam funded by oil-money, the clash caused by the spread of interest in mysticism, and calls for social justice and world justice have all presented challenges to the thought and practice of Muslims worldwide.

Page 176: The solid gold door of the Ka'bah, covered by its gold-embroidered curtain.

Fears of 'Islamofascism'

Fundamentalism is the desire to adhere to the teachings of the Qur'an and *sunnah* in a manner as close as possible to that taught by the Prophet Muhammad. Many Muslims feel that the centuries from his time to this have introduced all sorts of inaccuracies into what was intended as a perfect programme for life – wrong emphases, uncalled-for novelties – with a huge morass of scholarship making it impossible for the ordinary person to cope with it all. Fundamentalists long for the simplicity of life as they believe it to have been in Madinah.

This does not imply a rejection of science or technology, however, as Muslims were ordered to seek knowledge from cradle to grave, from every source possible. Muslims maintain that the Qur'an is compatible with any scientific process, and that modern knowledge and discoveries can only confirm its truths.

Inevitably, where Muslims live in society that has gone blatantly awry from the basic Islamic teachings, they are not comfortable and seek to improve matters. Where so-called Muslim rulers are corrupt, rapacious, cruel and prey to sexual sin, they are despised and inevitably feel threatened by the purists they govern. Some Muslim regimes, such as the Taliban, were excellent at destroying opium production, but curtailed female education and concentrated on such issues as beards and *burqas*. Some maintain traditional cultural customs rather than Islamic practices, such as forced marriages and female genital mutilation.

Khilafah

The yearning for the Islamic way of life has led many to long for a state of *khilafah*, the re-establishment of a Caliph of all Islam who would be the ruler of all Muslims around the globe. Some Muslim activists have felt that the Muslim world has been drifting, without aim or motivation, and have created sects devoted to reinvigorating the missionary urge – often aimed at those who are already Muslims. Most of the world's governmental systems do not favour mixing politics with religion, and can easily find examples of so-called Islamic government which has been very far from being either Islamic or a good thing. This does not stop the urge for *dawah* (mission and preaching), encouraging conversions, including these days by networking and use of the Internet.

The longing for a Caliph has gone through various stages – significantly from pan-Arabism (which does not appeal to the vast majority of Muslims who are not Arabs) to pan-Islam (which is not based on countries and borders, but believing individuals). The models of the USA, USSR and EU have suggested the possibility of a Union of Islamic States, if only it could be worked out. However, the 'divide and rule' policies of those who fear Islamic unity have so far proved effective.

must know

Islam has flourished as faith and practice during times of no caliph, rival caliphs and multiple caliphs – and in spite of inferior and 'secular' caliphs.

Jihadism and Islamofascism

'Islamofascism' is usually used to mean radical Islamism, and/or to describe the push by some Islamist clerics to impose their version of religious orthodoxy on the state and citizenry. As it happens, the brutal dictatorships, feudal monarchies, and corrupt military-run states in the Muslim world are, in fact, often America's allies.

'Jihadism' describes the beliefs and actions of Muslims of a certain type who aspire to 'win the world for Allah' but are prepared to force their way upon others, or hurt those they feel are 'against Islam' (i.e. *their* type of Islam). They are prepared to ignore the mainstream of their own faith in order to attack non-Muslim buildings, installations and personnel. This is a nightmare for the Muslim orthodox, who do not condone terrorism at all, especially when it involves killing innocent people (including other Muslims), committing suicide, destroying valuable infrastructure, and so on.

Islam has always counted within its ranks Muslims of all sorts – dry-as-dust scholars, flamboyant preachers, mystical dreamers, intellectual giants, those who favour puritanical simplicity, and the vastly wealthy who can patronize and cultivate the arts and crafts. It also includes those who feel that they alone are doing things the right way, and that everyone who disagrees with them, or slips into some sin or moral inadequacy, has 'left' Islam and can therefore be branded a *kafir*, destined for Hell.

Tariq Ramadan (b. 1962) is a leading modern reformer, a Swiss Muslim academic, and grandson of Hassan al-Banna, founder of the Muslim

Brotherhood. He believes that Muslims in Europe have to engage in European society. European Muslims must re-examine the fundamental texts of Islam and interpret them in light of their own cultural background, influenced by European society.

Divisive sexual issues

Muslims now live in societies in which promiscuity before marriage is regarded as normal and adultery seems to be condoned (both frequently presented in family TV drama), in which marriages break down at the least provocation, and people prefer to live together without 'risking' marriage at all, and in which it is illegal to object to homosexuality (which may even be explained to young children in school rather than regarded as something not to be paraded in public).

Some Muslim parents have made the mistake of overreacting; some have tried to force marriages on youngsters, others have punished severely (even by death – the so-called 'honour' killing) girls who have begun talking to, fraternizing with, 'dating' or seeking relationships with males before marriage. There is an urgent need for qualified and experienced imams to give counsel both to the young and to their parents in these situations.

Muslims are required to accept the laws of the country they live in, and where those laws are in opposition to Islamic law, decisions have to be made. In the UK, those married polygamously in countries where this is permissible have their marriages counted as valid, and divorces are not called for – but Muslims may not contract bigamous or polygamous marriage *in* the UK.

must know

The Prophet taught that there was a greater and a lesser *jihad*. The greater was the *jihad* of the heart, the struggle against one's ego.

Some Muslims perform 'religious' *nikahs* without registering the marriages legally, and might do this polygamously. This leaves the women totally unprotected in law, since a man may not have two common-law wives; and the offspring of such unions are illegitimate.

Issues of gender equality

Feminism and the role of women in Islam have come under much scrutiny, mainly from Muslim women themselves. The campaigns for gender equality and women's rights actually stem from the Qur'an itself and the Prophet's own teaching and example, and it was very obvious in his own day how the struggle was on to convince chauvinistic men of the need for change in their attitudes.

Several issues particularly involve women – abortion, femicide, female genital mutilation, forced and false marriages, child marriage, cousin marriage and temporary marriage (*mut'ah*). In fact, none of these practices is Islamic. Faith must be separated from the cultural norms and style of a particular society. Female genital mutilation is still practised in certain pockets of Africa and Egypt, and forced marriages may take place in certain Indian, Pakistani and Bangladeshi communities, but something that is a rule for Muslim women is a rule in Islam everywhere. These practices horrify Muslim women from other backgrounds.

Female imams?

All the functions of an imam, such as religious teaching, and spiritual and social counselling, have always been open to Muslim women, but they are not allowed to lead prayers where there are men in the congregation (although they may lead women only).

Those who hope to see the introduction of fully fledged female imams refer back to the case of the Prophet's friend, the scholarly Umm Waraqah, who had permission from him to lead her own household in prayers. Since her household included men, this is used to support the claim that women can lead men in prayer. However, most scholars regard this as an invalid deduction.

In recent years, the Muslim Hui people of China have begun building mosques solely for women, with women trained as imams in order to serve them. Efforts have been made to establish similar mosques in India and Iran. In fact, everywhere women are obliged to pray in separate buildings from the men this has in effect created separate mosques for them in which they may soon prefer to have their own leaders rather than follow an on-screen imam they cannot actually see. Others feel the need to return to the Madinah practice, of both sexes praying together in the same space.

In 1994, Amina Wadud became the first woman in South Africa to deliver the Friday *khutbah*, at the Claremont Main Road Mosque in Cape Town.

In early 2005, Sr Amina (now a professor of Islamic Studies at Virginia Commonwealth University, USA) led a congregation in Friday prayer in New York, sponsored by the Muslim Women's Freedom Tour, and by the website 'Muslim WakeUp!' (www.muslimwakeup.com).

did you know?

In 2004, Yasmin Shadeer led a mixed-sex congregation for the *isha* prayer in Etobicoke mosque in Toronto, Canada – the first recorded occasion in contemporary times. The United Muslim Association is determined to continue this practice, having women delivering the *khutbah* and leading the *salah*.

Sectarian and interfaith issues

Muhammad was said to have prophesied that his people would divide into 72 sects, and warned his followers: 'Truly, Satan is the wolf for humanity just as the wolf is for a flock. He seizes the solitary sheep going astray from the flock or going aside from the flock. Avoid the branching paths; it is essential for you to remain along with the community.' Sects certainly came fast into Islam's history.

'So set your face steadily and truly to the Faith... Turn back in repentance to Him and ...be not among those who join gods with Allah, [or] those who split up their religion and become sects, each party rejoicing in that which is with itself!' (Surah 3:30-32).

Some 90 per cent of Muslims are Sunni, and are considered to be mainstream traditionalists. About 10 per cent are Shi'ite, and both divisions subdivide into many, many groupings.

Both Sunnis and Shi'ites strenuously maintain that they alone are right in their understanding of Islam, and both regard themselves as 'al-Muminun', or the 'true believers'. Shi'ites believe in the divine right of the successors of Ali. His rightful successor is now concealed, but will appear at the end of the world as the 'Mahdi', the one rightly guided by Allah and thus able to guide others.

Shi'ism is broken into three main sects: the Twelve-Imam (Persia, Iraq, Afghanistan, Lebanon, Pakistan, and Syria), the Zaydis (Yemen) and the Isma'ilis (India, Iran, Syria, and East Africa). Each group has differences of doctrine.

The Twelvers (Ithna Ashiri) are by far the largest group. They believe that the line of Ali became extinct with al-Askari, the Twelfth Imam, who mysteriously disappeared in 873 CE. They believe that he will re-appear shortly before the end of the world.

The Zaydis (also Zaidi, Zaiddiyah, or 'Fivers') are the most moderate of the Shi'a groups and the nearest to the Sunnis in theology. According to Zaydi political theory, after Ali, Hasan and Husayn the imamate was open to whoever of their descendants established himself through armed rebellion. The Zaydis do not believe in the infallibility of their special imams, nor that they received divine guidance, or that the imamate must pass from father to son, but believe it can be held by any descendant of Ali.

The Isma'ili (or 'Seveners') are the second largest sect. They formed in the ninth century when a dispute arose concerning the successor to the Sixth Imam, Ja'far as-Sadiq. They believe in the coming of a messiah known as the 'Mahdi', who will establish a kingdom of righteousness on the earth and take vengeance for the oppression of the family of Ali. One historic Mahdi claimant was the Sudanese Muhammad Ahmad (1844–85) whose soldiers killed General Gordon at Khartoum. Isma'ili teach a gnostic-type theology, and have made many converts. Their current temporal leader is Aga Khan IV, and their present living Imam is Shah Karim al-Husayni.

Some other sects

The Babis follow the teachings of Ali Muhammad (1821–50) who claimed to be the *Bab* (Gate), and forerunner of the returned 12th Imam. He was executed, and his group split into two – Azalis and Baha'is. The Baha'is believe that Mirza Hussayn Ali

must know

The test of an individual's loyalty towards Islam lies in his or her chosen name. A Muslim is a Muslim – but if the Muslim prefers to be identified by the name of a group, sect or division, then they represent that sect rather than Islam.

known as Baha'ullah (d.1892) was the predicted prophet, the 12th Imam returned, as well as the Christ. Baha'is are not now counted as Muslims but as a separate faith group.

The Deobandi Movement, a Sufi Islamic revivalist movement founded in 1866, developed as a reaction to British colonization in India, which was felt to be corrupting Islam. It has now spread to other countries, such as Afghanistan, South Africa and the UK. Deobandis belong to the Sunni Hanafi school of thought. The Taliban are reputed to follow a strict and simplistic version of this school's teachings. According to *The Times* (online, 7 September 2007): 'the ultra-conservative movement, with modern roots in Pakistan's extremist *madrassahs*, now controls more than 600 UK mosques. It runs 17 of Britain's 26 Islamic seminaries, and they produce 80 per cent of home-trained Muslim clerics.'

The Barelwis were founded by Sayyid Ahmad Barelvi (1786–1831). His followers accepted Sufism, and opposed the Deobandis for their condemnation of several practices which are common in the Indian subcontinent, such as visiting graves, belief in the intercession of the spirits of dead saints for help, the use of amulets, over-venerating the Prophet and saints, etc. Their other fierce opponents are the Salafis in Saudi Arabia. Both groups call themselves the *Ahle Sunnah Wal Jamaah*.

The Alawis (also called Nusayris, Namiriya or Ansariyya) claim to be Muslims, but are not considered so by many Muslims, as their religion contains elements of other faiths, such as Christianity. Many of the tenets of their faith are secret, and they do not discuss their faith with outsiders. Slightly over 1 million of them live in Syria and Lebanon.

The Ahmadiyyahs (also known as Qadiani and Mirzai) were founded in 1980 when Mirza Ghulam Ahmad claimed to be the Mahdi, the promised Messiah and the likeness of Krishna. He also claimed to be a direct descendant of Jesus, who survived crucifixion and died in Kashmir. They are very active in the UK and run an excellent publications business. Their motto is 'Love for all, hatred for none.' Their Baitul Futuh mosque in London can accommodate 10,000 worshippers and is one of the largest in Western Europe.

The Salafis advocate a puritanical and legalistic stance in matters of faith and religious practice. Salafism is in general opposed to Sufism and Shi'ism, which are regarded as heresies. They see their role as a movement to restore Islam from what they perceive to be innovations, superstitions, deviances, heresies and idolatries.

The Tablighi Jama'at originated in India in 1838, founded by Muhammad Ilyas. Their main aim is to bring spiritual awakening to Muslims throughout the world. They concentrate on personal study and faith practices, and sacrifice their time in mission work mainly aimed at other Muslims.

Relationships with Jews and Christians

Many who believe in God are hopeful that the 21st century may see a 'coming together in peace' of all three 'Abrahamic' believers. They can see the ideal of those who worship God being allies instead of enemies, over and against the world of those who believe in no God. Those in favour of unity believe

must know

The mysterious grave of a prophet called Isa (Jesus) is preserved at a shrine called the Rozabel in Srinagar, India.

want to know more?

• **Elizabeth Warnock Fernea**, *In Search of Islamic Feminism*, **Anchor Books, 1998**
• **Elizabeth Warnock Fernea and Shemeem Burney Abbas**, *The Female Voice in Sufi Ritual: Devotional Practices in Pakistan and India*, **Anchor Books, 2003**
• **Ruqaiyyah Waris Maqsood**, *What every Christian should know about Islam*, **Islamic Foundation, 2000; and** *Mysteries of Jesus*, **Oxford, 2000**
• **Tariq Ramadan**, *Western Muslims and the future of Islam*, **2004;** *To Be a European Muslim*, **1999; and** *Islam, the West, and the Challenge of Modernity*, **2001**
• **Ismail al-Faruqi**, *Islam and Other Faiths*, **2000**

that the Prophet himself called for this when he asked the 'People of the Book' to come to that which was common amongst them. They believe that the God of the Jews, Christians and Muslims is the same One True God (however perceived), with the same chain of prophets, moral code, and hopes for eternal life.

Others, the more extreme devotees of their faiths, maintain that there is no way that Jehovah, or God the Father, or Allah, can be equated, and concentrate on the doctrinal differences to anathematize each other.

In an age where materialism and atheism are flourishing, there is still an innate human longing for faith. It remains to be seen which direction this will take in future.

Glossary

Ahkam - (plural. of *hukm*) laws, values and ordinances

Amal - actions in life resulting from one's beliefs

Amir al-Muminin - Commander of the faithful, a title given to Muslim leaders

Apostasy - a believer abandoning and turning against God

Ayah - a sign or miracle; one verse of the Qur'an

Caliph (Khalifah) - a deputy, or ruler on behalf of the real Ruler (in Islam - God); an elected leader of all Islam

Dhikr - remembering God, practices used in meditation

Din - (pronounced *deen*) the faith of Islam

Du'a - private and personal prayers and supplications as opposed to the set ritual prayers

Dunya - the things of this world, the temptations that can lead us astray

Eid ul-Adha - the feast of sacrifice that comes at the end of the Hajj

Eid ul-Fitr - the special feast that ends the month-long fast of Ramadan

Fatwa - a new legal decision given by a qualified scholar

Five Pillars - the five religious disciplines of Islam: *shahadah*, *salah*, *sawm*, *zakah* and Hajj.

Hadith - a recorded saying or teaching of the Prophet, indicating his practice and things he approved or disapproved

Hadd laws (pl. *Hudud*) - laws with specific judgements concerning *zinah* (adultery and fornication), *qadhf* (slander, false accusation), *sariqah* (theft), *hirabah* (taking with force, kidnapping, armed robbery, terrorism), *sukr* (consumption of alcohol) and *riddah* (apostasy).

Hafiz (f. *hafizah*, pl. *huffaz*) - someone who has learnt the entire Qur'an by heart

Hajj - the pilgrimage to Makkah

Halal - that which is permitted or allowed

Haram - forbidden, or sacred. Usually refers to forbidden foods and conduct.

Harem - the forbidden or private quarters in a house where people may not enter without invitation, set aside for the womenfolk and children of the family

Hujr al-aswad - the ancient black stone set in the Ka'bah, probably a meteorite

Ihram - to be in the state of *haram*, 'forbidding yourself' or separating yourself from the world in a 'sacred' condition

Ihsan - the realization for yourself that God exists

Ijma - consensus of opinion of learned jurists

Ijtihad - 'exertion', the effort a jurist makes to deduce a law from its sources

Imam - the prayer-leader; often an official position at a mosque although any male Muslim may lead the congregation. Women may lead other women.

Iman - a person's faith

Islam - the religion of submission to the will of God

Isma'ilis - a sectarian group following the seventh Shi'ite Imam, Isma'il. The Aga Khan is the present leader.

Istislah - consideration of public interest and justice when considering new laws

I'tikaf - state of separation from the world, for contemplation. Men may withdraw to the mosque, and women withdraw from their normal family life.

Jahannam - Hell, the eternal state of punishment in the afterlife, usually described in terms of torment, suffering and despair, but actually beyond our ability to comprehend; it may refer to complete annihilation, or may last 'as long as God wills'.

Jannah - Paradise or heaven, the eternal state of reward in the afterlife, usually described in terms of a peaceful garden, full of love and happiness - but in fact, beyond our powers of comprehension.

Jihad - to struggle or strive to do God's will in any aspect of life; also used to describe 'holy war' for the sake of restoring a just peace.

Jinn - a non-human being with free will,

said to be 'made of fire' (as humans are 'made of earth'), who can cause trouble or possess unfortunate people.

Khilafah – (i) the concept of having a Caliph of all Islam, (ii) the concept of responsible care of our planet on God's behalf

Laylat al-Miraj – the night of the Prophet's ascent through the heavens

Laylat al-Qadr – the Night of Power, the night on which the Prophet received the first revelation

Mahr – an agreed payment of money or property given by a husband to the woman he is about to marry.

Makruh - abominable, reprehensible, a course of conduct which is not forbidden but is disapproved if done

Mandub - recommended, praiseworthy; a course of conduct which is not an obligation but earns moral reward if done

Masjid – a mosque, a place for *sujud* or bowing down in worship

Nabi – a prophet or messenger of God, but one who has not been given an inspired text

Nikah - Islamic marriage contract.

Polygamy – having more than one spouse at the same time

Prophet – a person sent as a messenger by God

Purdah – the system of women living separated from non-family males

Qayamah – Day of Judgement

Qiyas – analogical reasoning aimed at extending a given ruling

Qisas - retaliation in kind (eye for an eye).

Quds – 'the holy', the site of the Jewish Temple at Jerusalem

Qur'an – the Muslim sacred text, the complete text of the Revelation

Rakah – a complete unit of prayer, the cycle of eight positions adopted during *salah*

Rasul – a prophet who has received an inspired text from God which can be written down

Risalah – prophecy, i.e. receiving messages sent from God via a human spokesman

Salah – the Muslim ritual prayer said five times daily, with set movements and words.

Sawm (or *siyam*) – fasting, i.e. no food, drink or sex from first light of dawn until sunset.

Shahadah – declaration of belief in God and His Prophet Muhammad

Shari'ah – the 'way' of the Prophet, Islamic Law

Shaytan (or Iblis) – the Devil, Satan, the chief *jinn*

Shi'ites (the Shi'at Ali, party of Ali, or Shi'a) – those Muslims who accepted Ali as first Caliph, and hold special beliefs about his descendants

Shirk – division of the unity of God; belief that anything has power like God, or over God

Sirah – study made of the life history of the Prophet

Sufism – Islamic spirituality and mysticism

Sujud – bowing in prayer with the head on the earth

Sultan – an independent ruler of a territory, under the supreme Caliph

Sunnah – the example of the Prophet's life and practice; Sunni Muslims are the majority, those who follow the mainstream of Islam

Surah ('something enclosed') - a chapter of the Qur'an

Takfir – the practice of branding those Muslims who disagree with you as unbelievers

Tarawih ('pauses') – special prayers in Ramadan during which the entire Qur'an is recited

Tawhid – the Unity, Oneness, and Absolute Supremacy of God

Twelve Imams - In Shi'ite Islam, the first 12 spiritual leaders of Islam after the Prophet, all his descendants

Ulama (pl. of *alim*) – the learned, knowledgable people in Islam.

Umm al-Kitab – the 'Mother of Books', the Qur'an

Umrah – a 'lesser' pilgrimage to Makkah, i.e. one made outside the Hajj time

Wudu – a special wash to bring about a state of ritual purity

Wuquf – the 'Stand before Allah' at Mt Arafat during the Hajj

Zakah – a 40th of surplus wealth, the portion given up for God's sake in order to 'purify' one's wealth.

Index

Figures in *italics* indicate captions.

Abbasid dynasty 88, 93, 135-8
abortion 104, 108, 114, 115, 182
Abraham 10, 11, 20
Abu Bakr 12, 17, 18, 20, 26, 28, 32, 36, 84, 134
Abu Talib 12, 13, 18, 19
Adam 76-7
adultery 103, 108, 109, 181
Afghanistan 178
afterlife (*akhirah*) 49, 58-61
Aghlabids 136
Ahmadiyyahs (Qadiani, Mirzai) 187
Aishah (the Prophet's widow) 19, 20, 26-7, 84, 134-5, 161
Alawis 186-7
alcohol 103, 108, 110, 126, 128
Alhambra, Granada, Spain 48, 64, 114, 155
Ali, Caliph 13, 17, 19, 20, 24, 28, 134-5, 142, 184
Allah/God
  the 'Beautiful Names' 49
  as creator 49-50
  infinite power of 96
  meaning of word Allah 6
  and miracles 29
  and polygamy 120
  relationship with human beings 50-51
  used by all Arabic speakers 48
  without gender 51
Almohads 137
Almoravid dynasty 137
angels 49, 51, 52-3, 70, 161
animal sacrifice/slaughter 87, 115, 126-7
apostasy 108, 109, 110
al-Aqsa Mosque, Jerusalem 98
arabesques 157, 169, 174
Arabia 6, 10, 11, 95
Arafat
  Mount 78, 80
  plain of 77, 80
architecture, Islamic 154-6, 156
art, Islamic 157, 160-62
Ashura, Day of 85, 87-8
Ataturk, Kemal 147
ayatollahs (leading Shi'ite imams) 108
Ayyub (Job) 87
Azalis 186

al-Azhar University, Cairo 158
Babis 185-6
Baghdad, Iraq 135, 137, 138, 143, 157, 160, 163
Baha'is 185-6
Baitul Futuh mosque, London 187
al-Baqi cemetery 84
Barelwis 186
bearing witness 63, 64-6
behaviour 103-5, 125-6
belly dancing 168
Bible, the 40
Bilal 18, 32
bin Laden, Osama 151, 178
birth 114-15
Bismallah ceremony 116
blasphemy 27, 29, 48
Blue Mosque, Istanbul 94
Burj Dubai, United Arab Emirates 156
Byzantines 137, 142, 143
Caliphs 134-8, 154, 161, 174, 179
calligraphy 157-8, 160, 169
carpets 96, 174-5
castles 156, 161
CE (Christian Era) 10
ceramics 172-4
charity 104, 115, 120
childhood 116-17
China 183
Christianity, Christians 11, 135, 138, 156, 186, 187-8
circumcision 115-16, 116
  female 116, 179, 182
civil war, Islamic (*fitna*) 134-5
clothing 27, 127, 127
'Code of 19' 42-3
Constantinople (later Istanbul) 142-3
contraception 104-5, 114
conversion to Islam 118
Córdoba, Spain 32, 93, 170, 174
crafts, Islamic 168-75, 170, 171
crescent moon (symbol of Islam) 95
Crimean War (1853-6) 147
Crusades 137-8, 171
Damascus, Syria 135, 138
dance 166-8, 167
death 58, 121, 123-5
death penalty 109, 110, 130
Delhi Sultanate 136
Deobandi Movement 186
destiny (fate) 49, 56

divorce 104, 117, 119, 121, 181
Dome of the Rock, Jerusalem 21, 95, 98, 134, 145, 171
domes 92, 93, 94, 95, 96
drama 158
Egypt 137, 138, 147, 162
Eid ul-Adha ('Feast of Sacrifice') 77, 84, 85, 87
Eid ul-Fitr (feast at the end of Ramadan) 72, 85-7
environment 131
Etobicoke mosque, Toronto, Canada 183
euthanasia 123
Eve 76-7
evolution 146
exploitation (*riba*) 130
extremism 23, 35, 107, 149, 151
Fabrics 169
family 114
Farabi, Abu Nasr 163-4
fasting 63, 65, 72-3, 85 6, 89
Fatimah (the Prophet's daughter) 19, 84, 111
Fatimids 136, 162
fatwa (legal opinion or verdict) 106, 162-3
femicide 115, 182
feminism 182
festivals 85-9, 95
film 162-3
Five Pillars of Islam 63, 64, 65, 95, 103
Flood, the 87
forts 156
free will 56-7, 59
fundamentalism 42, 107, 147, 177, 178
funerals 123, 124-5
Gender equality 182-3
Genghis Khan 138, 141, 157
ghazals ('songs of yearning') 166, 168
Ghaznavids 136
Ghurids 136
glass 171
God *see* Allah/God
Great Mosque, Damascus, Syria 10, 93
Hadhramawt, Yemen 55
hadiths 11, 14, 32, 34, 102, 110, 136, 164
hafiz, huffaz 34, 36, 73
Hajarah 77
Hajj 12, 26, 37, 63, 65, 74-81,

76, 81, 84, 84, 85, 87, 98, 159
halal 126, 127, 128
haram 76, 78, 103, 104, 118, 126, 128
Heaven (*Jannah*) 19, 58-61, 88, 114
Hell (*Jahannam*) 19, 58-61, 180
hijab 127-8, 127
hijrah 20-21, 33
history of Islam 133-51
  China and South-East Asia 139, 141
  the Crusades 137-8
  Islam in the Maghreb 139
  the Mamluk sultanate 138
  the Mongols 138, 139
  the Gunpowder Empires 141-4
  reformers 144
  Saudi Arabia and Wahhabism 144-7
  the spread of 133, 135-9, 141
  the succession - Sunni and Shi'ite 134-5
  the 20th century 147-50
  1967-present 150-51
homosexuality 108, 117, 181
'honour' killing 181
House of the Tree, Baghdad 170
Husayn (Muhammad's grandson) 88
Hussein, Saddam 151
Ibn Taymiyyah 144-5
Ibrahim 76, 77, 84, 87, 116
Ibrahimi mosque, Hebron 171
imams 68, 68, 97, 98, 124, 135, 146, 181
  female 182-3
India 136, 137, 149, 161, 169, 183, 186
Iran 148, 150-51, 183
  Shah of (Mohammad Reza Pahlavi) 108, 151
Iran-Iraq War 151
Iraq 148
Isfahan, Iran 138, 154
Islamic Jihad terror group 149
Islamic law (Shari'ah law) 101-11, 136
  basis of 102-5
  the five categories 103-5
  hadd laws 107-11
  madhhabs (schools of jurisprudence) 103-5, 107
Islamofascism 180
Isma'il 76, 77, 87

Isma'ilis 185
Israel 149, 150
ivory 169, 170
Jamaat-e-Islami 150
Jerusalem 19, 88, 136, 138
Jesus 10, 18, 20, 21, 27, 56, 88, 187
Jews 10, 22, 24, 115, 135, 187-8
Jibril (angel Gabriel) 6, 9, 13-15, 19, 26, 31, 35, 52, 53, 77, 89
jihad 181
Jihadism 180
jinn 53-4
Judgement, Day of 49, 58, 59, 65, 88, 108, 135
Ka'bah (Great Mosque), Makkah 11-12, 20, 26, 66, 77-80, 84, 98, 123, 125, 178
kafirs (unbelievers) 149, 180
Khadijah (Muhammad's first wife) 13, 14, 17, 19
Khalifa, Dr Rashid 42-3
Khomeini, Ayatollah Ruhullah 108, 150-51
King Hassan II Mosque, Casablanca, Morocco 95
Kuwait 151
Law of Moses 109
Laylat ul-Bara'at 89
Laylat ul-Miraj 88-9
Laylat ul-Qadr 73, 89
literature and learning 157-60
London Muslims 97
lunar calendar 85, 95
Madinah 20-24, 84, 87, 183
Constitution of 22
madrassahs (schools) 98-9, 157, 186
Maghreb 139
'Mahdi' (messiah) 184, 185, 187
Makkah 11, 15, 19, 20, 23-6, 33, 74, 75, 76, 80, 135, 159
direction of (qiblah) 64, 69, 70, 92, 97, 125
pilgrimage to, see Hajj
Malcolm X 186
Mamluks 138, 143
Al-Mansur 93
marriage 117-20, 179, 181, 182
Mary, mother of Jesus 35, 52
Maududi, Maulana 150
meat, halal 126
Mecca see Makkah
Medina see Madinah
metalwork 171-2
Mevlana Rumi's mosque, Qonya, Turkey 94, 166
mihrab 96, 97, 98
Milad an-Nabi 88
Mina, valley of 80, 81
minarets 94, 95
minbars 96, 98
miracles 29, 56
Mongols 138, 139, 162

monotheism 11-12
Moses 10, 20, 35, 56, 87
mosques 22, 68, 73, 86, 89, 91-9, 92, 93, 94, 103
art 157, 161
external and internal features 94-8, 96
main types of 92-4
what mosques are used for 98-9
for women 183
mothers 114
mu'adhins 95, 97
Mu'awiyyah 134, 135
Mughal Empire 95, 141-2, 154, 161, 169
Muhammad
God's Messenger 6, 9, 27, 31, 35
early years 12
marriage to Khadijah 13
call to prophethood 13-15
mission in Makkah 15-17
reaction to his message 17-18
leaves Makkah 19
ascension 19-20, 21, 88-9
Hijrah: migration to Madinah 20-21, 87
Muslim state and charter 22
ruler of Madinah 22-3
the life of prayer 23
wars 23-5
the year of the deputations 25
victory over Makkah 25-6
the death of the Prophet 26-7
the sunnah - his example 27-9, 102, 110
the seal of the prophets 56
and the Hajj 76
birthday 88
and film 162-3
Muhammad, Ali 185-6
Muharram 85
muqarnas 174
music 163-6, 165
Muslim Brotherhood 148, 149, 180-81
Muslims: definition 6, 18
names 115
Nation of Islam 186
nature 131
Nike 45
Nuh (Noah) 87
oil 150, 156
old age 121, 123
OPEC (Organization of the Petroleum Exporting Countries) 148
Organization of Islamic Conference (OIC) 182
Ottoman Empire, Ottomans 93, 138, 142-4, 147, 148, 161, 162, 170
Pakistan 149, 178, 186

palaces and mausoleums 154-5
Pan-Arabism 147, 179
Pan-Islamic Movement 146, 147
Peacock Throne of Shah Jahan 170
'People of the Book' 135, 188
Persia (later Iran) 136, 138, 155, 161, 163, 164
poetry 158-9
polygamy 120, 181, 182
pork, eating 103, 126
poverty 129
prayer 20, 22, 23, 63, 65, 66-71, 66, 67, 68, 104
beads (tasbih) 71
five daily prayers (the salat) 66, 68-9
Friday prayers 71, 97, 183
funeral 123, 124
imams 68, 68
individual prayers 70, 71, 109, 147
personal prayers (du'at) 66, 71
prayer halls 93, 94, 96-7, 99
the prayer sequence 69-70
prayer times 68-9, 96, 97, 172
prayer-mats 66, 66
preparation for 66-7
wudu 67-8, 67, 71, 116
prophecy (risalah) 49, 55-6, 57
Prophet's Mosque, Madinah 28, 98
punishments 109-11
al-Qaeda 149, 151
qiblah see under Makkah
Qur'an 6, 15, 26, 27, 29, 31-45, 98, 99, 102, 104-7, 125, 144, 161, 164, 178, 182
Qutb, Sayyid 149, 150
Ramadan 33, 35, 72, 73, 85, 89
Ramadan, Tariq 180-81
Resurrection, Day of 56, 58, 59, 125
Rushdie, Salman 106
Safavid empire 142, 143, 161
Saladin 137-8
Salafis 186, 187
Satan (Shaytan, Iblis) 54-5, 76, 77, 81, 81
Saudi Arabia 147, 151, 168, 186
science 145-6
sects 184-7
Seljuk Turks 136, 137
September 11 2001 attacks 151, 163
sexual immorality 108, 109, 117
Shari'ah law see Islamic law
Shi'a Islam, Shi'ites 28, 85, 88, 105, 106, 134, 135, 159, 166, 184-5, 187
Six Day War (5-10 June, 1967) 150
socialism, Arab 149, 150

Sokoto caliphate, Nigeria 139
soul (nafs) 50-51, 52, 58-9
Spain 135, 137, 163
spirit (rouh) 51-2
star, five-pointed 95
stoning the symbol of Satan 81, 81, 84
stuccowork 173-4
Sufism, Sufis 50, 88, 133, 138, 139, 141, 160, 164-8, 186, 187
suicide 123, 180
suicide bombings 57, 150
Suleyman the Magnificent 143-4, 155
Suleymaniya Mosque, Istanbul 155
sultans 138, 161, 162
sunnah 27-9, 102, 103, 105, 106, 110, 121, 144, 178
Sunni Islam, Sunni Muslims 85, 88, 103, 105, 134, 135, 184, 186
surah, surat 16, 33, 35
Tabligh Jama'at 187
Taj Mahal 154-5
takfir 149, 180
Taliban 151, 178, 179, 186
tawhid (the One-ness of God) 48-9
taxation see wealth sharing
terrorism 43, 108, 150, 177, 180
textiles 169
theft 108, 109
Thousand and One Nights, The 160
tiles 94, 96, 154, 155, 171, 173
Timur (Tamerlane, Tamburlaine) 142
travelogues 159-60
Turkey 147, 161, 164, 165
Twelve-Imam sect 184, 185
Umar, Caliph 36, 84, 87, 134
Umayyad dynasty 93, 135, 137, 161
United Muslim Association 183
Uthman, Caliph 36-7, 84, 134
Wahhab, Muhammad ibn Abdu'l 144, 145
Wahhabi sect 84, 125, 168
wealth 129-30
sharing (zakah) 25, 63, 65, 73-4, 130, 135
whirling dervishes 165, 167, 168
wood 169-70, 170
work 128-9
World Trade Centre, New York 151
World War I 147
World War II 148
wudu 67-8, 67, 71, 97, 116
Zamzam water 78
Zayd ibn Harithah 13, 17, 36
Zaydis 184, 185